Instructor's Manual and Test Bank to Accompany

— FIFTH EDITION —

TEN STEPS *to* IMPROVING COLLEGE READING SKILLS

John Langan

ATLANTIC CAPE COMMUNITY COLLEGE

TP

Books in the Townsend Press Reading Series:

Groundwork for College Reading with Phonics
Groundwork for College Reading
Ten Steps to Building College Reading Skills
Ten Steps to Improving College Reading Skills
Ten Steps to Advancing College Reading Skills
Ten Steps to Advanced Reading

Books in the Townsend Press Vocabulary Series:

Vocabulary Basics
Groundwork for a Better Vocabulary
Building Vocabulary Skills
Building Vocabulary Skills, Short Version
Improving Vocabulary Skills
Improving Vocabulary Skills, Short Version
Advancing Vocabulary Skills
Advancing Vocabulary Skills, Short Version
Advanced Word Power

Other Reading and Writing Books:

Everyday Heroes
English at Hand
English Essentials
Voices and Values: A Reader for Writers

Supplements Available for Most Books:

Instructor's Edition
Instructor's Manual and Test Bank
Online Exercises

Copyright © 2008 by Townsend Press, Inc.
Printed in the United States of America
9 8 7 6 5 4 3 2 1

ISBN-13: 978-1-59194-110-1
ISBN-10: 1-59194-110-5

**For book orders and requests for desk copies or supplements,
contact us in any of the following ways:**

By telephone: 1-800-772-6410

By fax: 1-800-225-8894

By e-mail: cs@townsendpress.com

Through our website: www.townsendpress.com

CONTENTS

TEST BANK   43

Note: There are four mastery tests for each skill, supplementing the six mastery tests in the book itself. These tests can be used at a variety of points along the student's path of working through the chapter and the mastery tests in the book.

NOTES FOR INSTRUCTORS

On the first three pages of the Instructor's Edition of *Ten Steps to Improving College Reading Skills*, Fifth Edition, I list some hints for teaching a reading course and for using the book. I add here some other comments.

Using a Class Contract

In the first class of the semester, I explain to students that I regard the course as a serious, professional relationship between them and me. I say that I want them to sign a professional contract for taking the course. I then pass out a contract for them to read and sign.

In my experience, the contract helps motivate younger students in particular to come to class and to assume responsibility for their own learning. Some of the older students don't need such a contract, but they welcome a clear presentation of basic ground rules regarding attendance and grading in the course.

A copy of the contract appears on pages 6–7; you have permission to modify and use this contract in whatever way you see fit.

Supplements for the Book

There are three supplements for the book:

1   An *Instructor's Edition,* which is identical to the student book except that it provides the answers to all of the practices and tests.
2   The combined *Instructor's Manual and Test Bank,* which you are now reading.
3   *Online exercises* consisting of at least two additional mastery tests for each skill plus two combined-skills tests—23 tests in all. These online tests are free for students and instructors using the book and may be accessed at **www.townsendpress.com**.

If you've adopted the book for use in your reading classes, you're entitled to free copies of any of these supplements. Call 1-800-772-6410 or e-mail us at **cs@townsendpress.com** to get them shipped out to you immediately.

A Suggested Syllabus

Weeks 1–10:

One way to begin using the book is to have students work through the activities in "How to Become a Better Reader and Thinker" on pages 3–9. Then, as the first homework assignment, ask them to read the essay "Reading for Pleasure and Power" on pages 10–14. Discuss the questions on page 14 in the next class and urge students to take advantage of the book offer on page 15.

I suggest then teaching one chapter a week, following the order in the book. Generally at the end of a chapter I give two mastery tests: one for practice and one that counts for a grade.

I go over the tests in class right after students take them. (I recommend collecting test papers as students finish and distributing them to students in other parts of the room. Some students resist putting X's on a paper that belongs to the person sitting right next to them.) That way students get immediate feedback on how they have done. Also, after class all I need to do is to check the grades quickly and transfer them to my grade book.

As the semester progresses, I use additional mastery tests, every so often, to review previous skills covered in the class.

Weeks 11–15:

In the last five weeks, students read two selections a week from Part Two of the book. They also do the remaining mastery tests, including some of the tests in this manual, as well as the combined-skills tests in the book and in this manual.

Having done all of the reading of the materials in the book, as well as all of the thinking required to complete the many activities, students are, in my experience, better readers and thinkers. They are better equipped both to handle a standardized reading test at the semester's end and to go on to content courses in their college curriculum.

Suggested Answers to the Discussion Questions

Pages 23–42 in this manual provide suggested answers to the discussion questions that follow each of the twenty readings in Parts One and Two of the book. There was simply no room in the Instructor's Edition for this material.

Writing Assignments

Writing and reading are closely related skills: practice at one will make a student better at the other. Also, writing about a selection is an excellent way of thinking about it. For these reasons, three writing assignments are provided (beginning on page 599 of the book) for each of the twenty reading selections in Parts One and Two.

If you ask students to write about a selection, I suggest you first have them read the "Brief Guide to Effective Writing" that appears on pages 597–598.

Teaching Vocabulary

One basic change that I've made in my teaching of reading is that I now directly teach vocabulary. We all know that students don't know enough words. Because they don't, they have trouble understanding what they read, and they're limited in what they can write. (We have all seen how, in standardized reading tests, students are frustrated because they don't know enough of the words in a passage to understand it and to answer comprehension questions about it. And we all know that because of the vocabulary problem, the standardized tests that are intended to measure reading comprehension are often in fact serving as vocabulary tests.)

I teach vocabulary using a words-in-context approach (it is of no value to ask students to memorize isolated lists of vocabulary words). Specifically, I use a book titled *Improving Vocabulary Skills, Short Version*, by Sherrie Nist and Carole Mohr. There are twenty chapters in this book, with ten words in each chapter. I do the first chapter in class, so that students understand how to use the pronunciation key for the words and understand just how the chapter works. I then assign one or two chapters a week for homework.

In class each week, I walk around and check students' books to see that they have worked through the four pages of material for each chapter. (After this quick check, I then return the focus of the class to reading skills.) Every third week, I give students one of the several tests that follow each unit of five chapters in the book. My vocabulary syllabus looks like this:

Week 2:   Vocabulary chapter 1 covered in class
Week 3:   Vocabulary chapters 2–3 for homework
Week 4:   Vocabulary chapters 4–5 for homework plus a test on Unit One in class
Week 5:   Vocabulary chapters 6–7 for homework
Week 6:   Vocabulary chapters 8–9 for homework
Week 7:   Vocabulary chapter 10 for homework plus a test on Unit Two in class
Week 8:   Vocabulary chapters 11–12 for homework
Week 9:   Vocabulary chapters 13–14 for homework
Week 10: Vocabulary chapter 15 for homework plus a test on Unit Three in class
Week 11: Vocabulary chapters 16–17 for homework
Week 12: Vocabulary chapters 18–19 for homework
Week 13: Vocabulary chapter 20 for homework plus a test on Unit Four in class

The Importance of Continual Reading and Thinking

Continual reading—coupled with thinking about what one has read—is the very heart of a reading class. *One improves the skills of reading and thinking by guided reading and thinking.* This statement is emphasized with good reason. If a teacher is not careful, he or she may play too participatory a role in the classroom, getting more reading and thinking practice than the student does. The teacher should serve as a manager, using the materials in the text to give students the skills practice they need. *Ten Steps to Improving College Reading Skills* helps the teacher ensure that students do a great deal of active reading and thinking in the classroom.

The Importance of Constant Feedback

Along with continual reading, writing, and thinking, it is vital that students get frequent feedback. Here are ways they can secure such feedback:

- Small-group interactions
- Class discussions and reviews
- Short one-on-one sessions with the instructor
- Graded quizzes and tests
- The Limited Answer Key in the back of the book
- The online exercises available at **www.townsendpress.com**

In addition, since instructors using *Ten Steps to Improving College Reading Skills* as a class text are permitted to reproduce any or all parts of this manual, you can selectively hand out copies of answers included here.

All of the exercises in the book are designed to make it easy to give clear and specific feedback. If students are going to learn to read and think more effectively, then they need clear, logical, specific responses to their efforts. This book enables teachers to provide such feedback.

Outlining, Mapping, and Summarizing

To take thoughtful, effective study notes, students need to learn three essential techniques: outlining, mapping, and summarizing. All three techniques often require students to identify the main idea and the major supporting details of a selection. But while educators agree that these three techniques are important for students to learn, they are all too seldom taught.

The book gives students instruction and practice in all three techniques. Passages in the "Supporting Details" and the two "Relationships" chapters, as well as all of the reading selections in Part Two, are followed by an outline, a map, or a summary activity. To complete many of these activities, students must look closely at the basic organization of the selection. They must think carefully about what they have read by asking two key questions: "What is the point?" and "What is the support for that point?" As students apply the techniques from one selection to the next and get specific feedback on their efforts, they will develop their ability to think in a clear and logical way.

Readability Levels . . . and Their Limitations

Below are the readability grade levels for the text of the book itself and the twenty reading selections. Because the book has been prepared on a computer, and there are now software programs that determine readability, it has been possible to do a complete readability evaluation for each reading, rather than merely sampling excerpts from the materials.

Please remember, however, that there are limits to the reliability and validity of readability scores. For instance, a readability formula cannot account for such significant factors as student interest, prior knowledge of a subject, the number of examples provided to explain concepts, and the overall clarity and logic of the writing.

Thus, while "The Scholarship Jacket" has a readability level of 5th grade, it is a sophisticated adult piece that may be more challenging to students than, for example, "Students in Shock," which has a reading level of 10. And while "Child-Rearing Styles" has a readability level of 12, it is so clearly organized that it is a piece that developmental students can manage to understand. I respect readability levels, but I also take them with a grain of salt, and I have kept other factors in mind while determining the sequence of readings.

Material	Word Count	Reading Level
Text of *Ten Steps*		8
Part One		
1. Night Watch	663	7
2. Here's to Your Health	1076	9
3. Child-Rearing Styles	487	12
4. Rowing the Bus	2034	6
5. Wonder in the Air	685	9
6. Students in Shock	1160	10
7. Gender Inequality in Health Care and in the Workplace	1246	9
8. The Scholarship Jacket	1950	5
9. In Praise of the F Word	960	8
10. Gambling—A Dangerous Game	1882	8

Material	Word Count	Reading Level
Part Two		
1. The Yellow Ribbon	927	7
2. The Certainty of Fear	1722	9
3. Shame	1774	6
4. The Bystander Effect	1578	9
5. "Let's Roll."	2537	7
6. Coping with Nervousness	1261	9
7. Compliance Techniques	1560	10
8. Lizzie Borden	1028	9
9. Nonverbal Communication	961	10
10. The Power Within	4171	8

A Final Note

Writing a book that contains hundreds of explanations and activities is a bit like being in a ball game where one steps up to the batter's box an almost countless number of times. One tries to get as many hits and extra-base hits as possible: to explain every concept so that students really understand it; to provide readings and practices that both interest students and teach the skills. One tries not to hit any foul balls. Hopefully there are not too many in this Fifth Edition of a book that has benefited from a great deal of teacher and student feedback.

Realistically, though, you might find that despite my best efforts, some items may not work. If they don't, and/or if you or your students are confused or uncertain about certain items, let me know so that I can consider making changes in the next printing or revision of the book. Send a note to me at Townsend Press, 439 Kelley Drive, West Berlin, NJ 08091. Alternatively, call Townsend Press at its toll-free number: 1-800-772-6410; send a fax to 1-800-225-8894; or send e-mail to **cs@townsendpress.com**; your comments will be passed on to me. And if you have a question, a Townsend editor will get back to you with an answer very shortly.

My thanks in advance for your help in my effort to keep improving the book!

John Langan

A PROFESSIONAL CONTRACT

FOR FIFTEEN WEEKS TOGETHER

between

_____

(Student's name here)

and

_____

(Instructor's name here)

Welcome to *(name of course)* _____. Counting today, we will be spending fifteen weeks together. How successful we are will depend on how well we follow a business contract that I would like you to read and sign, and that I will then sign and return to you. Here are the terms of the contract.

MY ROLE IN THE CONTRACT

My role will be to help you practice and master important reading and writing and thinking and learning skills. I will try to present these communication skills clearly and to give you interesting and worthwhile practice materials. I will conduct this as a skills course—not a lecture course where you could borrow a friend's notes afterwards. Typically several skills will be explained briefly in class, and you will then spend most of the class time practicing those skills, making them your own. You will be learning in the best possible way: through doing.

Why learn these skills?

I promise you that the skills will be of real value to you in all the other courses you take in college. They will make you a better reader, writer, thinker, and learner, and they can dramatically increase your chance for success in school.

The skills can be just as valuable for the career work you are likely to do in the future. Consider that America is no longer an industrial society where many people work on farms or in factories. Instead, most jobs now involve providing services or processing information. More than ever, communication skills are the tools of our trade. This course will be concerned directly with helping you learn and strengthen the communication skills that will be vital for job success in the 21st century.

YOUR ROLE IN THE CONTRACT

Experiencing the course

Your role in this contract will be to come to every class and to give a full effort. Much of the value and meaning of this skills course will come from what happens in class, so you must be here on a steady basis. Imagine trying to learn another skill without being present: for example, imagine learning how to drive without the *experience* of actually being in the car and working with the controls and getting feedback from your instructor. How much would you learn about the skill of driving if you relied only on the notes of a classmate? In a similar way, to really learn communication skills, you need direct experience and practice. So if you miss classes, you are in effect missing the course.

Shaping your attitude

Some people start college with a "high-school mindset." They are passive; they do the minimum they need to get by; their attention is elsewhere; they are like the living dead—and the American high-school system (and watching thousands of hours of television) may be to blame. Gradually these people realize that college is not high school: they don't have to be in college, and they are no longer part of the sad game played out in many high schools, where they receive a free ride and promotion no matter how little they do.

If your attitude about learning has been hurt by what happened in high school, then part of your role is to change your attitude. You can do so, and this contract will help.

Understanding sick days and personal days

You should try not to miss *any* classes. But in the professional environment of this class, like in the work world, everyone is entitled to a set number of sick days as well as "personal days"— unexplained absences. In this course, you will have a total of *(insert number)* _____ such days— which can cover such real-world happenings as sickness, car breakdowns, or even the death of someone you know. If you missed more than this amount of time in a real-world job contract, you would be let go. (Only in some extraordinary situation, such as an extended illness confirmed by a doctor's report, might an exception apply.) The professional terms of the work world will apply here: if you miss more than _____ classes, you cannot pass the course.

YOUR ROLE IF YOU MISS CLASS

If you do miss a class, you are responsible for getting the homework for the following week's class. To do so, call a classmate. Write down the names and phone numbers of two people in the room. (For now, use the people sitting on either side of you; you can always change these names later.)

Classmate # 1: *Name* _____   *Phone* _____

Classmate # 2: *Name* _____   *Phone* _____

Note that you **must** turn in all homework assignments or you **cannot pass the course**.

If a test or tests are given on a day you miss class, you cannot ordinarily make up these tests. Instead, you will receive a grade of M (Missing) for each missed test. When all your grades are averaged at the end of the semester, three M's will be omitted; the rest will convert to zeros.

YOUR COMMITMENT

I've read this contract, and the terms seem fair to me. (I like the fact that this college class is being treated as a professional situation, and I'm learning the ground rules up front.) I accept the responsibility and the challenge to make this course worth my time and money.

_____   _____

Signed by (your name here)   *Date*

_____

Witnessed by the instructor

OR: If you don't want to sign this, please meet with me after this class to talk about why.

ANSWERS TO THE TESTS IN THE BOOK

Answers to the Review and Mastery Tests in Part One

VOCABULARY IN CONTEXT:
Review Test 1
1. context   4. B
2. A   5. definition . . .
3. C   examples

VOCABULARY IN CONTEXT:
Review Test 2
A. 1. B   C. 6. D overjoyed
   2. B   7. E provided
B. 3. B   8. A discouraged
   4. A   9. C nag
   5. B   10. B doubtful

VOCABULARY IN CONTEXT:
Review Test 3
(Wording of answers may vary.)
A. 1. practical
   2. clean
   3. reveal
   4. relieve
   5. at the same time
B. 6. looked down upon
   7. guilty
   8. tried
   9. add to
  10. joined

VOCABULARY IN CONTEXT:
Review Test 4
1. B   6. A
2. D   7. C
3. D   8. D
4. B   9. D
5. A   10. C

VOCABULARY IN CONTEXT:
Mastery Test 1
A. 1. A   D. 7. C
B. 2. D   8. B
   3. B   E. 9. A
   4. C   10. B
C. 5. search
   6. false name

VOCABULARY IN CONTEXT:
Mastery Test 2
A. 1. A   6. modest
B. 2. B   D. 7. C
   3. A   8. C
C. 4. plain   E. 9. D
   5. conduct   10. B

VOCABULARY IN CONTEXT:
Mastery Test 3
1. A   6. D
2. C   7. D
3. C   8. C
4. C   9. D
5. B   10. B

VOCABULARY IN CONTEXT:
Mastery Test 4
1. C   6. C
2. C   7. A
3. A   8. D
4. B   9. B
5. D   10. C

VOCABULARY IN CONTEXT:
Mastery Test 5
A. 1. C
   2. D
   3. C
   4. A
   5. C
B. *(Wording of answers may vary.)*
   6. cut off
   7. give a false account of;
     misrepresent; twist
   8. come between;
     get involved
   9. required
  10. became more forgiving;
     gave in

VOCABULARY IN CONTEXT:
Mastery Test 6
A. 1. D die
   2. B deadly
   3. F forced to experience
   4. G give credit for
   5. J reducing
B. 6. E most common
   7. I stir up interest
   8. J uncontrolled
   9. D increased
  10. F passed

MAIN IDEAS:
Review Test 1
1. B   4. A
2. B   5. other material
3. A   in the paragraph

MAIN IDEAS:
Review Test 2
A. 1. A. S
      B. S
      C. S
      D. P
   2. A. S
      B. S
      C. P
      D. S

B. 1. A. SD
      B. SD
      C. T
      D. MI
   2. A. SD
      B. SD
      C. T
      D. MI

MAIN IDEAS:
Review Test 3
1. 1
2. 3
3. 9
4. 2
5. 2

MAIN IDEAS:
Review Test 4
1. D   6. A
2. C   7. B
3. A   8. D
4. A   9. B
5. C   10. A

MAIN IDEAS:
Mastery Test 1
A. 1. A. P
      B. S
      C. S
      D. S
   2. A. S
      B. P
      C. S
      D. S
   3. A. S
      B. S
      C. S
      D. P

B. *Group 1*
   A. SD
   B. T
   C. SD
   D. MI
   Group 2
   A. T
   B. SD
   C. MI
   D. SD

MAIN IDEAS:
Mastery Test 2
A. 1. A. S
      B. P
      C. S
      D. S
   2. A. S
      B. S
      C. S
      D. P
   3. A. P
      B. S
      C. S
      D. S

B. *Group 1*
   A. SD
   B. SD
   C. T
   D. MI
   Group 2
   A. MI
   B. T
   C. SD
   D. SD

MAIN IDEAS:
Mastery Test 3
1. 1
2. 2
3. 6
4. 1
5. 2

MAIN IDEAS:
Mastery Test 4
1. 3
2. 2
3. 1
4. 7
5. 2

MAIN IDEAS:
Mastery Test 5
1. 6
2. 4
3. 2
4. 1
5. 2

MAIN IDEAS:
Mastery Test 6
1. 2
2. 1
3. 2
4. 3
5. 11

SUPPORTING DETAILS:
Review Test 1
1. specific . . . specific   4. mapping
2. T   5. condense
3. supporting details

SUPPORTING DETAILS:
Review Test 2
A. *Main idea:* Several factors *influence the justice system's treatment of criminals.*
  1. Sex of offender affects severity of sentence 2
    b. Court more reluctant to send mother to prison than father 4
  2. Race is another factor 5
    a. Nonwhites get parole and probation less often 6
    b. Blacks executed more often for capital crimes 7
  3. a. Young offenders given special treatment 9
B. 8. C   9. C   10. B

SUPPORTING DETAILS:
Mastery Test 1
A. *Main idea:* Divorce has serious negative consequences.
  1. a. Starting to date again can be nerve-racking.
  2. Emotional difficulties among original family members are common.
    a. Husband and wife feel guilt and resentment.
  3. Financial adjustments are necessary.
    a. Alimony, child support, and property disposal must be dealt with.
B. 7. B   8. A   9. C
  10. They can undo complicated bolts on gates.

SUPPORTING DETAILS:
Mastery Test 4
A. *Main idea:* Researchers have come up with a number of theories to explain the functions of sleep.
  1. Gives body time to repair brain cells and create chemical that makes brain think
  2. Enables body to save energy
  3. Keeps people out of trouble
  4. Reduces memory
B. 6. C
C. 7. A
  8. B
  9. B
  10. C

SUPPORTING DETAILS:
Review Test 3
A. *Main idea: Serious depression has definite warning signs.*
  1. Change in sleep patterns
  2. Abnormal eating patterns
  3. Trouble thinking or concentrating
  4. General feeling of hopelessness
B. *Main idea:* There are three common ways that people deal with their feelings.

Withhold them	Display them	Describe them

C. 10. C

(In all these tests, wording of main ideas and supporting details may vary.)

SUPPORTING DETAILS:
Mastery Test 2
A. 1. A   4. C
  2. B   5. A
  3. A   6. A
B. *Main idea:* Three types of human memory allow us to remove or keep information as needed.
  1. Sensory memory
  2. Short-term memory—stores about 7 items for about 30 seconds
  3. Long-term memory—stores enormous numbers of items for a long period

(In all these tests, wording of main ideas and supporting details may vary.)

SUPPORTING DETAILS:
Mastery Test 5
A. 1. B   4. B
  2. C   5. C
  3. A
B. *Main idea:* Experts in our country have suggested various purposes of imprisonment.

Punishment	Rehabilitation	Deter crime	Keep criminals off streets

SUPPORTING DETAILS:
Review Test 4
1. B
2. A
3. D
4. A
5. long interviews
6–10. A. 1. Basic temperament the child is born with
      2. Early emotional environment
    B. 1. Authoritative
      2. Authoritarian
      3. Permissive

SUPPORTING DETAILS:
Mastery Test 3
A. 1. A   4. B
  2. B   5. B
  3. A   6. C
B. *Main idea:* Chimpanzees use objects in their environment as tools.
  1. Sticks to catch termites and steal honey
  2. Leaves as drinking cups, for cleaning, and as sponges
  3. Stones to crack open nuts

SUPPORTING DETAILS:
Mastery Test 6
A. 1. b. Informal and friendly atmosphere in the Senate
  2. Procedural differences
    a. House rules—many and complex
    b. Senate rules—short and simple
  B. Political outlook of members
    1. Representatives concerned with local issues
B. *Main idea:* A number of conditions stimulate aggression.

Pain	Attacks	Crowding

IMPLIED MAIN IDEAS:
Review Test 1

1. implied   4. central point
2. topic   5. sometimes
3. support

IMPLIED MAIN IDEAS:
Review Test 2

A. 1. B
   2. A
B. 3. Watching TV has several benefits.
   4. Lower-class criminals are not treated as well as higher-class criminals.

(In all these tests, wording of implied main ideas may vary.)

IMPLIED MAIN IDEAS:
Review Test 3

A. 1. B
   2. D
B. 3. Several techniques can help you get a good night's sleep.
C. 4. C

IMPLIED MAIN IDEAS:
Review Test 4

1. B   6. D
2. C   7. A
3. C   8. A
4. A   9. D
5. A   10. B

IMPLIED MAIN IDEAS:
Mastery Test 1

1. D
2. A
3. C
4. D

IMPLIED MAIN IDEAS:
Mastery Test 2

1. B
2. C
3. D
4. A

IMPLIED MAIN IDEAS:
Mastery Test 3

A. 1. A
   2. D
B. 3. There are several positive ways to encourage your family to exercise more often.
C. 4. D

IMPLIED MAIN IDEAS:
Mastery Test 4

A. 1. D
   2. D
B. 3. B
   4. A

IMPLIED MAIN IDEAS:
Mastery Test 5

A. 1. B
   2. B
B. 3. Several tips will help you do better on exams.
   (Wording of answer may vary.)
C. 4. C

IMPLIED MAIN IDEAS:
Mastery Test 6

A. D
B. D

RELATIONSHIPS I:
Review Test 1
1. the relationships between
2. addition
3. time
4. T
5. supporting details

RELATIONSHIPS I:
Review Test 2
A. 1. B before   6. E second
   2. A also B. 7. B
   3. D one   8. After
   4. F then   9. A
   5. C final   10. also

RELATIONSHIPS I:
Review Test 3
A. 1. After *A*   6. B
   2. First *C* B. 7. B
   3. Then *E*   8. A
   4. As *B*   9. B
   5. later *D* 10. A

(In all these tests, wording of main ideas and supporting details may vary.)

RELATIONSHIPS I:
Review Test 4
1. B   6. C
2. C   7. C
3. B   8. B
4. D   9. A
5. C   10. B

RELATIONSHIPS I:
Mastery Test 1
A. 1. A After B. 6. after
   2. C Another   7. next
   3. B also   8. Last
   4. D Moreover 9. then
   5. E Then   10. B

RELATIONSHIPS I:
Mastery Test 2
A. 1. E When B. 6. B
   2. C First C. 7. First
   3. D Then   8. also
   4. B Before 9. Finally
   5. A also   10. A

RELATIONSHIPS I:
Mastery Test 3
A. 1–5. 3, 1, 4, 2, A
B.   6. B
C.   7. A
  8–10. *Main idea:* Prevention against injury involves a combination of two types of preventive measures.
    1. Active prevention— methods that require people to do something to reduce the risk of injury
    2. Passive prevention— methods requiring little or no action on the part of those being protected

RELATIONSHIPS I:
Mastery Test 4
A. 1–4. 4, 1, 3, 2
    5. B
B.   6. B
C. *Main idea:* Work shapes human lives in fundamental ways.

Consumes enormous amounts of time   Gives life structure and rhythm   Causes stress

RELATIONSHIPS I:
Mastery Test 5
A. 1. B
   2. in 1849 (*or* After *or* Then *or* finally)
B. 3. A
   4. C
C. 5. B
  6–10.

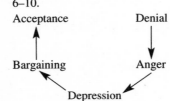

Acceptance   Denial
Bargaining   Anger
Depression

RELATIONSHIPS I:
Mastery Test 6
A. 1. B
   2–3. *Any two of the following:* First, Next, Third, Finally
B. 4. A
   5. also
   6. A
C. 7. A
  8–10. *Main idea:* Children learn their gender roles in three main ways.
    2. Imitation
    3. Self-definition

RELATIONSHIPS II:
Review Test 1
1. examples
2. comparison
3. contrast
4. C
5. C

RELATIONSHIPS II:
Review Test 2
A. 1. B effects
    2. D just like
    3. C However
    4. A Because
    5. E such as

B. 6. B
   7. C
   8. A
   9. C
   10. A

RELATIONSHIPS II:
Mastery Test 1
A. 1. B For example
    2. D Just as
    3. E Therefore
    4. A Because
    5. C In contrast

B. 6. A
   7. C
   8. C
   9. B
   10. A

RELATIONSHIPS II:
Mastery Test 4
A. 1–4. 4, 1, 3, 2
    5. A
B. 6. A
   7. B
   8. result
C. 9. B or C
   10. C or B

(In Tests 5 and 6, wording of main ideas and supporting details may vary.)

RELATIONSHIPS I and II:
Mastery Test 1
A. 1. D Then
    2. C for example
    3. B First
    4. A cause
    5. E unlike

B. 6. D However
   7. A After
   8. B As a result
   9. C For instance
   10. E next

RELATIONSHIPS II:
Review Test 3
A. 1. A
    2. For instance *or* for example
B. 3. C
    4. alike *or* But *or* while *or* In contrast
C. 5. B
    6. because *or* As a result *or* effect
D. 7. A
    8. example
E. 9. B
    10. affected *or* Because *or* result

RELATIONSHIPS II:
Mastery Test 2
A. 1. B
    2. reason *or* As a result
B. 3. C
    4. In contrast
C. 5. A
    6. For example
D. 7. B
    8. causing *or* Since *or* leads to *or* causes
E. 9. C
    10. different *or* not . . . different *or* contrasts *or* Nevertheless *or* same *or* alike *or* similar

RELATIONSHIPS II:
Mastery Test 5
A. 1. B
    2–5. To learn to do their jobs better
         To get a raise or promotion
         To learn a new field
         To learn for the sake of learning
B. 6. B
    7–10. *Good manager*
        4. Is flexible
       Poor manager
       1. Is surprised by problems
       3. Takes on extra tasks
       4. Clings to old rules

RELATIONSHIPS I and II:
Mastery Test 2
A. 1. C
    2. but *or* yet *or* however *or* Still
B. 3. C
    4. reason *or* due to *or* causes
C. 5. A
    6. When *or* Then *or* As *or* Now *or* After
D. 7. B
    8. For instance *or* example
E. 9. B
    10. One *or* Another *or* third

RELATIONSHIPS II:
Review Test 4
1. B
2. D
3. B
4. A
5. A
6. C
7. C
8. C
9. B
10. A

RELATIONSHIPS II:
Mastery Test 3
A. 1–4. 3, 2, 4, 1
    5. C
B. 6. C
    7. differently *or* in contrast *or* while
C. 8. D
    9. A
    10. example

RELATIONSHIPS II:
Mastery Test 6
A. 1. C
    2–6. Delays
         Lack of resources
         Losses
         Failure
         Discrimination
B. 7. B
    8–10. *Main idea:* Role conflict—a situation in which the different roles an individual is expected to play make incompatible demands.

| For a working mother, the expectations of motherhood may conflict with those of a full-time job. | For a priest, the responsibility to treat confessions confidentially may conflict with his responsibility to the community. |

RELATIONSHIPS I and II:
Mastery Test 3
A. 1. C
B. 2. B
C. 3. A
D. 4. A
E. 5. B

INFERENCES:
Review Test 1

1. suggested
2. useful
3. useful
4. T
5. tell . . . show

INFERENCES:
Review Test 2

A. 1, 3, 5, 7
B. 2, 4, 6, 7
C. 1, 2

INFERENCES:
Review Test 3

A. 1, 3, 5, 6
B. 5. A
   6. A
   7. B
   8. A
   9. A
   10. C

INFERENCES:
Review Test 4

1. B
2. D
3. C
4. C
5. C
6. A
7. B
8. D
9. D
10. B

INFERENCES:
Mastery Test 1

A. 1, 4, 6
B. 2, 3, 4
C. 1. 2, 5
   2. 1, 5

INFERENCES:
Mastery Test 2

A. 1, 4, 5
B. 1, 3, 6
C. 7. C
   8. B
   9. A
   10. C

INFERENCES:
Mastery Test 3

A. 3, 4, 6
B. 4, 5, 6
C. 7. A
   8. B
   9. C
   10. A

INFERENCES:
Mastery Test 4

A. 1. C
   2. C
   3. C
   4. B
   5. A
B. 6. A
   7. A
   8. C
   9. B
   10. B

INFERENCES:
Mastery Test 5

A. 2, 4, 5, 6, 8, 10
B. 1, 3, 5, 8

INFERENCES:
Mastery Test 6

A. 2, 3, 5, 6, 9
B. 6. B
   7. A
   8. C
   9. A
   10. A

PURPOSE AND TONE:
Review Test 1

1. purpose	6. opposite
2. inform	7. B
3. entertain	8. C
4. persuade	9. C
5. attitude	10. B

PURPOSE AND TONE:
Review Test 2

1. P	4. I
2. I	5. P
3. E	

PURPOSE AND TONE:
Review Test 3

1. D
2. E
3. C
4. F
5. A

PURPOSE AND TONE:
Review Test 4

1. D	6. B
2. C	7. C
3. B	8. B
4. A	9. A
5. D	10. C

PURPOSE AND TONE:
Mastery Test 1

A.	1. I	B.	6. C
	2. P		7. B
	3. E		8. E
	4. P		9. D
	5. E		10. A

PURPOSE AND TONE:
Mastery Test 2

A.	1. I		6. I
	2. P		7. P
	3. E	B.	8. D
	4. I		9. C
	5. P		10. E

PURPOSE AND TONE:
Mastery Test 3

A.	1. H		6. E
	2. G		7. F
	3. D	B.	8. I
	4. B		9. P
	5. A		10. E

PURPOSE AND TONE:
Mastery Test 4

A.	1. C		6. I
	2. D		7. J
	3. E	B.	8. I
	4. F	C.	9. C
	5. H		10. B

PURPOSE AND TONE:
Mastery Test 5

A.	1. B	C.	5. B
	2. C		6. D
B.	3. A	D.	7. C
	4. D		8. D

PURPOSE AND TONE:
Mastery Test 6

A.	1. A	C.	5. B
	2. A		6. A
B.	3. A	D.	7. A
	4. B		8. D

ARGUMENT:
Review Test 1
1. C   4. B
2. A   5. D
3. C

ARGUMENT:
Review Test 2
A. 1. B   B. 5. B
    2. B   6. D
    3. D   7. E
    4. C   8. A
                    9. D
                   10. F

ARGUMENT:
Review Test 3
A. 1. C
    2. A
    3. D
B. 4. D
    5. C

ARGUMENT:
Review Test 4
1. C   6. D
2. D   7. A
3. C   8. C
4. C   9. B
5. A   10. A. S
                B. P
                C. X
                D. S

ARGUMENT:
Mastery Test 1
A. 1. B   B. 5. A
    2. D   6. D
    3. C   7. E
    4. B   8. B
                    9. D
                   10. E

ARGUMENT:
Mastery Test 2
A. 1. A   7. A
    2. B   8. C
    3. B   9. F
B. 4. A   C. 10. D
    5. D
    6. E

ARGUMENT:
Mastery Test 3
A. 1. B
    2. D
B. 3. C
    4. D
    5. B

ARGUMENT:
Mastery Test 4
A. 1. A   B. 10. D
    2. C
    3. F
    4. C
    5. D
    6. F
    7. A
    8. C
    9. E

ARGUMENT:
Mastery Test 5
A. 1. A   B. 7. B
    2. D   8. B
    3. F   C. 9. A
    4. B   10. C
    5. C
    6. F

ARGUMENT:
Mastery Test 6
A. 1. B   B. 7. C
    2. D   8. D
    3. F   C. 9. D
    4. B   10. B
    5. C
    6. F

CRITICAL READING:
Review Test 1
1. A fact
2. A news report
3. a mixture of fact and opinion
4. Opinions
5. B   8. T
6. A   9. T
7. A   10. B

CRITICAL READING:
Review Test 2
1. O   6. F+O
2. F   7. F
3. F   8. O
4. O   9. F
5. O   10. O

CRITICAL READING:
Review Test 3
A. 1. B   B. 6. B
2. C   7. A
3. C   8. C
4. B   9. A
5. A   10. B

CRITICAL READING:
Review Test 4
1. A   6. A
2. D   7. B
3. A   8. B
4. T   9. B
5. D   10. A

CRITICAL READING:
Mastery Test 1
A. 1. O   B. 11. O
2. F   12. F
3. O   13. O
4. F   14. F
5. F   15. F
6. O   16. O
7. F   17. F
8. O   18. F+O
9. F   19. F
10. F+O   20. O

CRITICAL READING:
Mastery Test 2
A. 1. F   B. 11. O
2. O   12. F
3. O   13. F
4. F   14. F+O
5. F   15. F
6. O   16. F
7. O   17. O
8. F   18. F
9. F+O   19. F
10. O   20. O

CRITICAL READING:
Mastery Test 3
A. 1. A   B. 7. C
2. D   8. F
3. B   9. A
4. D   10. B
5. B
6. C

CRITICAL READING:
Mastery Test 4
A. 1. B   B. 7. F
2. D   8. F
3. A   9. C
4. C   10. B
5. D
6. C

CRITICAL READING:
Mastery Test 5
A. 1. B   B. 6. C
2. C   7. B
3. A   8. A
4. B   9. C
5. A   10. A

CRITICAL READING:
Mastery Test 6
A. 1. C   B. 6. A
2. B   7. C
3. A   8. B
4. B   9. A
5. C   10. C

Answers to the Reading Selections in Part Two

1   THE YELLOW RIBBON

Skills Questions

1. A	6. B	11. C	16. C
2. B	7. D	12. B	17. A
3. D	8. B	13. T	18. C
4. B	9. C	14. C	19. D
5. F	10. D	15. C	20. C

Summarizing

B

2   THE CERTAINTY OF FEAR

Skills Questions

1. B	6. A	11. C	16. D
2. B	7. B	12. A	17. C
3. C	8. D	13. D	18. B
4. D	9. A	14. A	19. C
5. B	10. B	15. A	20. C

Mapping

Childhood:	Midlife: time
the loss of	running out
something precious	
Adolescence:	Old age: frailty and
looking "stupid"	loss of independence

3   SHAME

Skills Questions

1. C	6. B	11. B	16. T
2. D	7. C	12. T	17. A
3. C	8. D	13. C	18. B
4. A	9. C	14. T	19. C
5. D	10. B	15. D	20. C

Outlining

A. Becomes ashamed of his poverty
   2. Is humiliated by teacher
   3. Leaves school and avoids it in the future
B. Becomes ashamed of his own failure to help another
   3. Offers to pay for meal, but too late

4   THE BYSTANDER EFFECT

Skills Questions

1. C	6. D	11. B	16. C
2. D	7. C	12. D	17. C
3. B	8. D	13. C	18. B
4. D	9. C	14. D	19. A
5. D	10. D	15. B	20. A

Summarizing *(Note: Wording of answers may vary.)*
witnesses present
no one called the police during the attack
the reactions of bystanders to emergencies
interpret
is felt by each member of the crowd

5   "LET'S ROLL."

Skills Questions

1. D	6. C	11. B	16. C
2. B	7. A	12. D	17. B
3. B	8. A	13. D	18. D
4. A	9. D	14. D	19. B
5. F	10. C	15. A	20. B

Outlining

A. *Introduction—paragraphs 1 to 4*
   1. Lisa Beamer's conversations with counselor and
      Airfone supervisor
B. Narrative of the events of Flight 93—
   paragraphs 5 to 31
C. *Conclusion—paragraphs 32 to 33*
   1. Lisa Beamer as hero's widow
   2. Teddy Roosevelt's words

6   COPING WITH NERVOUSNESS

Skills Questions

1. C	6. C	11. A	16. C
2. B	7. B	12. A	17. A
3. B	8. B	13. A	18. A
4. A	9. D	14. D	19. A
5. C	10. A	15. D	20. D

Outlining

B. People can learn to cope with the fear of public
   speaking.
C. There are various ways to cope with your nervousness
   about public speaking.
   2. Prepare adequately for your speech.
   4. Use certain techniques as you walk to the speaker's
      stand and just after.

7 COMPLIANCE TECHNIQUES

Skills Questions

1. C	6. C	11. D	16. C
2. D	7. D	12. C	17. A
3. A	8. D	13. B	18. B
4. A	9. C	14. D	19. D
5. B	10. C	15. B	20. D

Summarizing *(Note: Wording of answers may vary.)*

2. . . . making a smaller request. The first request is so outrageously large that people might be tempted to slam the door in the requester's face.
   Example: . . . to give a great deal of time.
3. asking a person to agree to something on the basis of incomplete information and then later telling the full story.
4. *Example:* At a bake sale, customers were more likely to buy cupcakes for 75 cents if they were told they would also get two free cookies.

8 LIZZIE BORDEN

Skills Questions

1. C	6. A	11. A	16. B
2. C	7. C	12. C	17. D
3. C	8. B	13. C	18. B
4. A	9. A	14. C	19. A
5. B	10. B	15. A	20. D

Summarizing

B

9 NONVERBAL COMMUNICATION

Skills Questions

1. B	6. A	11. B	16. A
2. B	7. D	12. T	17. B
3. C	8. D	13. B	18. D
4. D	9. A	14. A	19. A
5. A	10. C	15. B	20. B

Outlining *(Note: Wording of answers may vary.)*

A. Nonverbal messages: the use of personal space
   3. Social distance
   4. Public distance
B. 2. a. Helps communicate certain emotions, attitudes, and preferences
      b. Supports our verbal communications

10 THE POWER WITHIN

Skills Questions

1. C	6. B	11. C	17. B
2. B	7. A	12. A	18. A
3. D	8. D	13. D	19. B
4. D	9. B	14. C	20. C
5. C	10. C	15. B	

16. Dr. Martin Luther King wrote, "Life's most persistent and urgent question is, 'What are you doing for others?'"

Outlining *(Note: Wording of some answers may vary.)*

B. 2. "I'm too busy."
   5. "I'm bored with the subject."
C. 1. Have a dream.
   3. Have the determination and commitment to do the work.
   8. b. Increases the chances for job success.

Answers to the Combined-Skills Tests in Part Three

COMBINED SKILLS:
Test 1

1. C		5. B
2. D		6. C
3. B		7. A
4. C		8. D

COMBINED SKILLS:
Test 2

1. A		5. D
2. B		6. C
3. C		7. D
4. C		8. A

COMBINED SKILLS:
Test 3

1. B		5. D
2. D		6. A
3. C		7. B
4. B		8. A

COMBINED SKILLS:
Test 4

1. D		5. B
2. C		6. D
3. A		7. A
4. B		8. B

COMBINED SKILLS:
Test 5

1. B		5. A
2. D		6. B
3. B		7. A
4. B		8. C

COMBINED SKILLS:
Test 6

1. B		5. A
2. B		6. C
3. A		7. A
4. C		8. D

COMBINED SKILLS:
Test 7

1. B		5. D
2. A		6. B
3. D		7. C
4. C		8. D

COMBINED SKILLS:
Test 8

1. B		5. B
2. C		6. D
3. C		7. C
4. D		8. B

COMBINED SKILLS:
Test 9

1. A		5. C
2. B		6. B
3. B		7. C
4. D		8. B

COMBINED SKILLS:
Test 10

1. B		5. D
2. C		6. A
3. C		7. D
4. B		8. D

COMBINED SKILLS:
Test 11

1. C		5. C
2. C		6. C
3. B		7. D
4. B		8. D

COMBINED SKILLS:
Test 12

1. D		5. A
2. C		6. D
3. A		7. D
4. B		8. C

COMBINED SKILLS:
Test 13

1. C		5. A
2. B		6. B
3. D		7. B
4. C		8. D

COMBINED SKILLS:
Test 14

1. C		5. C
2. B		6. A
3. C		7. C
4. A		8. B

COMBINED SKILLS:
Test 15

1. C		5. B
2. B		6. A
3. A		7. D
4. C		8. B

COMBINED SKILLS:
Test 16

1. B	5. A
2. D	6. A
3. A	7. B
4. C	8. A

COMBINED SKILLS:
Test 17

1. B	5. A
2. D	6. B
3. C	7. A
4. D	8. B

COMBINED SKILLS:
Test 18

1. C	5. A
2. D	6. B
3. C	7. A
4. C	8. C

COMBINED SKILLS:
Test 19

1. B	5. A
2. D	6. A
3. A	7. D
4. C	8. C

COMBINED SKILLS:
Test 20

1. A	5. A
2. C	6. D
3. A	7. C
4. C	8. A

SUGGESTED ANSWERS TO THE DISCUSSION QUESTIONS IN PART ONE

Note: The numbers in parentheses refer to paragraphs in the reading. For some questions, additional related questions have been included to enhance class discussion.

1   NIGHT WATCH, Roy Popkin

1. When do you think the Marine realized that calling him to the hospital was a mistake? Was it when he first saw the old man or before? What parts of the reading support your conclusion?

The Marine's comment in paragraph 13 suggests that he knew there had been a mistake when he first saw the old man: "I knew right off there'd been a mistake, but I also knew he needed his son." This is stated as though he made the judgment at the hospital, upon seeing the man and perhaps realizing that nobody else was there to be with him as he died.

2. How do you think the dead man's real son felt about the other Marine being with his dying father? How would you feel?

Many readers will feel that the real son would have mixed feelings—great gratitude for the Marine's kindness, jealousy of a stranger who spent crucial time with his father, and sadness at having been denied the opportunity to be with his father one more time.

3. The incident in the reading took place because of some surprising coincidences. What were they? Has a surprising or interesting coincidence ever taken place in your life? If so, what was it, and how did it affect you?

The coincidences in the reading were "there had been two Marines with the same name and similar serial numbers in the camp" (14). Answers to the second and third question will vary.

4. By going out of his way for a stranger, the Marine showed "in a uniquely human way that there are people who care what happens to others." Have you ever gone out of your way to help a stranger? Or have you seen someone else do so? Tell what the situation was and what happened.

Answers will vary.

2   HERE'S TO YOUR HEALTH, Joan Dunayer

1. *Unfortunately, Tod's experience with alcohol is not so rare. Do you know anyone who has had a negative experience because of drinking or because of drinking and driving? Where was that person drinking, and how much did he or she have? Explain what eventually happened.*

    Answers will vary. (Students may also be able to draw upon the local news for stories of drinking and driving.)

2. *If it's true that "beer doesn't make anyone sexier," why do you think so many young people drink so much beer in social situations?*

    One important reason is that alcohol lowers inhibitions, giving young people the confidence they seek to relax among others and reach out for social connections, both romantic and otherwise. Another reason, of course, is that young people tend to feel peer pressure and thus behave as their peers do; if some in a group are drinking, others are likely to do so as well.

3. *Think about a wine, liquor, or beer ad you have seen in a magazine, in a newspaper, or on television. Which alcohol myth described in "Here's to Your Health" does that ad promote? What details of the ad contribute to that myth?*

    Students can discuss current ads on TV and in campus publications. Inevitably, all alcohol ads include one of the myths, perhaps most commonly the idea that alcohol makes one attractive to the opposite sex. Bringing magazine ads to class may enliven discussion on this question.

4. *Cigarette advertising is no longer allowed on television. Do you think beer ads should also be outlawed on TV? In college newspapers? Explain your answers.*

    Answers will vary, but students can address such issues as the causes and effects of drunk driving and the results of extensive student drinking, as well as alcohol companies' rights of expression.

3 CHILD-REARING STYLES, Diane E. Papalia and Sally Wendkos Olds

1. What type of parenting style did you grow up with? Would you say this style was effective? Why or why not?

To answer this question, students can look back at the specific elements of each type of parenting and think of examples from their own upbringing that fit a particular description. For instance, a student who states that his parents "set few rules" (permissive parents, 5) might tell about some behaviors that were allowed in his or her home that are unlikely to be allowed in other homes. Answers to the second and third questions will vary.

2. Why do you think Diana Baumrind feels that teaching by example is useful?

Baumrind obviously feels that children are greatly influenced by the behavior of adults in their lives. She would probably say that "Do as I say, not as I do" is not an effective approach with young people, who tend to learn their behavior, like their language, by imitating the adults in their lives.

Can you think of any adults whose example influenced you—either positively or negatively? How has a particular example influenced who you are today?

3. Baumrind encourages parents to show interest in children. What are some ways in which parents can show interest in children?

In considering this answer, students can think about how adults showed—or did not show—interest in them as they grew up. Following are a few of the numerous possible ways adults can show interest in children:

- Reading out loud to children and asking their opinions about what was read
- Discussing the events of the children's day at dinnertime
- Asking children for their opinion on various matters, such as what color their room should be painted, what they think of their teachers, and so on.

4. The authors feel that children are born with "their own inborn temperaments." Has your experience with children confirmed or contradicted their idea that children have different temperaments, starting from the time they are born? Give some examples.

Students can draw upon their experiences as siblings and/or parents. How alike or different were they from their siblings? How alike or different were their own children, or the children of someone close to them, from birth on?

4   ROWING THE BUS, Paul Logan

1. *Paul Logan titled his selection "Rowing the Bus." Yet very little of the essay actually deals with the incident the title describes—only the first and last paragraphs. Why do you think Logan chose that title?*

   Through his choice of title and by beginning with the rowing story and ending with a reference to it ("No one should have to row the bus"), Logan uses the image of rowing the bus to represent the cruelty and humiliation typical of situations involving bullies.

2. *Logan wanted to be kind to George, but he wanted even more to be accepted by the other students. Have you ever found yourself in a similar situation—where you wanted to do the right thing but felt that it had too high a price? Explain what happened.*

   Since bullies are everywhere, students are likely to have had experiences similar to Logan's. Thinking of bullies whom students have known may help jog their memories of relevant incidents.

3. *Logan refers to "a sinister code of childhood that demands there must always be someone to pick on." Why do children need someone to pick on?*

   Picking on someone allows a bully to feel stronger and better than that person—in his own eyes as well as in others'. This fact suggests that at least some bullies have fundamentally weak self-images.

4. *The novelist Henry James once said, "Three things in human life are important. The first is to be kind. The second is to be kind. And the third is to be kind." What do you think schools or concerned adults could do to encourage young people to treat one another with kindness, rather than with cruelty?*

   In addition to acting kindly themselves, teachers can use reading materials and school incidents to initiate discussions and raise students' consciousness about kindness.

   More specifically, what ways can you suggest to at least encourage young people not to bully? (Here are some things the schools can do to handle bullying: Use students and community volunteers to monitor playgrounds and lunchrooms and to help victims; provide martial-arts training to teach respect for others and self-confidence; institute a school policy making bullying an unacceptable offense.)

5 WONDER IN THE AIR, Jeff Gammage

1. *Was the author right to lie to his daughter? Why or why not?*

   Some students may agree with the author's original point of view—that a lie is a lie and is wrong, no matter how well-meant the lie is. Others will probably sympathize with his change of opinion and think he was right to tell his daughter that Santa Claus was real. Those students may say, for instance, that the belief in Santa Claus is a happy, innocent part of childhood that children should not be denied, and that children will give up their belief in Santa when they are ready to do so.

2. *When you were a child, did you believe in Santa Claus? How did you find out that he doesn't really exist?*

   Answers will vary. Encourage students to compare and contrast their experiences. Are the ones whose parents encouraged their belief in Santa happy that their parents did so? Was it traumatic for them to find out that Santa was not real?

3. *When or if you have children, will you encourage them to believe in Santa, the Easter Bunny, and the tooth fairy? Why or why not?*

   Answers will vary.

4. *The author and his wife decided that "no lies" would be their "one firm parental rule." What do you think are some other good parental rules?*

   Students might consider rules such as these: "We will not use physical punishment." "No smoking/ drinking/ drug use around the child." "Be respectful of the child and expect the child to be respectful back." "Behave as we want our child to behave." "Limit TV watching." Encourage students to discuss what they want their children to learn from the parental rules.

6   STUDENTS IN SHOCK, John Kellmayer

1. *If you were a peer counselor for Lisa or Dan, what advice might you give her or him?*

   Lisa's desperation suggests that she must first address her emotional problems, perhaps even leaving school temporarily to gain emotional strength. Once she has dealt with her depression, she can seek rational ways to handle her financial problems and to settle on a major. Good college counselors can help her with both problems.

   Dan would probably benefit greatly by doing just what he had thought of doing ("talking to somebody in the psychological counseling center," 5). If he had, he'd soon have realized that nothing is more "wrong with him" than with many other people struggling with a difficult situation. Like Lisa, Dan could also benefit from the guidance of a good vocational counselor.

2. *What were—or are—the most stressful parts of college life for you? Explain why. What ways have you found for dealing with that stress?*

   Answers will vary, but many of the students' stresses undoubtedly will generally resemble those mentioned in the reading. Aspects of college life to consider include forming and maintaining personal support systems, dealing with financial pressure, choosing a major, learning study skills, and keeping up with class work.

3. *Kellmayer writes that "colleges . . . are trying in a number of ways to help students cope with the pressures they face." What resources does your college offer? Have you tried any of them? How do you think your school could improve the services it offers to help students deal with "student shock"?*

   It may be helpful for the instructor to bring in materials explaining the counseling services available at the college and/or for a representative of the counseling services to come to class to explain what services are available and to answer questions. Students who have used some of the services at the college may wish to tell about their experiences, including whether or not they benefited and if so, how.

4. *On the basis of your college experience so far, what one piece of advice would you give to an incoming freshman?*

   Students can draw upon their answers to question 2 in answering this question.

7 GENDER INEQUALITY IN HEALTH CARE AND IN THE WORKPLACE, James M. Henslin

1. *Medical researchers discovered that men and women receive different health care because of "unintended sexual discrimination." How might such clear-cut discrimination be "unintended"? Do you know of any cases of gender health discrimination? Tell what happened.*

   Discrimination might be unintended if the medical professionals involved do not recognize what they are doing. If they are in the habit of thinking that women exaggerate their symptoms or "go running to the doctor for every little thing," they may not take a woman's complaint as seriously as they would a man's. They may not intend to harm the woman, but their action still leads to a harmful outcome. Answers to the rest of the question will vary.

2. *According to Henslin, women suffer and men benefit from gender discrimination in the U.S. work force. Have you ever experienced or witnessed gender discrimination at work? Tell what happened.*

   Answers will vary.

3. *Did it surprise you to learn that in modern U.S. society, women earn significantly less than men? Explain. In your opinion, what are the causes of the gender gap, and what do you think would have to happen for it to end??*

   Answers will vary.

8   THE SCHOLARSHIP JACKET, Marta Salinas

1. *In her first meeting with the principal, Marta could have challenged him by telling what she had overheard the two teachers saying. Why do you think she stayed silent? What do you think the principal would have said or done if she'd told him she knew the real reason she wasn't being given the jacket?*

There could be several reasons why Marta didn't tell the principal what she had heard. She may have been afraid of seeming disrespectful to the principal. She may have been afraid of angering him or the teachers. She may have felt a misplaced sense of shame over what she had heard. She may have felt it was taboo to talk to the principal about racism.

The principal would surely have been worried and embarrassed if he knew what Marta had overheard. He might have denied it, claiming that Marta had misunderstood. He might have taken his anger out on her, accusing her of eavesdropping. Or he might have been so ashamed that he agreed to give her the jacket.

2. *Why do you think the principal gave in during his second meeting with Marta? What do you think that shows about Marta's grandfather's decision? What do you think might happen when the principal has to face the Board again? If you were the principal, what would you have said to the Board?*

The principal apparently recognized the truth of what Marta said—that if the jacket were paid for, it wouldn't be a scholarship jacket. He knew in his heart that Marta deserved the jacket. Clearly, Marta's grandfather made the right decision.

The principal will be in trouble with the Board. The members of the Board, which include Joann's father, apparently are more concerned with keeping the "important" people in the community happy than they are in recognizing true scholarship. The Board might even threaten the principal's job.

Answers to the third question will vary, but it seems likely that the principal will tell the Board that as an educator, he has to see the scholarship jacket given to the student who has earned it.

3. *Marta implies that she was discriminated against because of her racial background (she was Mexican) and her family's economic condition (they were poor). Have you ever experienced discrimination, or do you know of a friend who has experienced it? Explain.*

Answers will vary.

4. *Marta stresses again and again how important the scholarship jacket was to her and how hard she worked to win it. Is there something you worked hard to achieve when you were younger? How long did you work toward that goal? How did you feel when you finally succeeded—or did not succeed? What lessons, if any, did you learn from the experience?*

Answers will vary.

9 IN PRAISE OF THE F WORD, Mary Sherry

1. *Do you know anyone who has failed or almost failed a course? What effect did the experience have on that person?*

   Answers will vary.

2. *Most people think of failing a course as a negative experience. Why, then, does Sherry consider the threat of failure to be a positive teaching tool? Do you agree?*

   Sherry states that "the threat of flunking . . . is an expression of confidence by both teachers and parents that the students have the ability to learn the material presented to them" (11). This contrasts with the common practice of passing students who haven't mastered the basic skills, a practice that is excused "by saying kids can't learn if they come from terrible environments" (8). Sherry obviously believes most students can learn and that passing them without their having learned basic skills "dooms them to long-term illiteracy" (11).

3. *People often look back on their education and realize that some of the teachers they learned the most from were their strictest teachers. Who do you think you learned more from, strict teachers or lenient ones? Give examples to support your point.*

   Answers will vary. A discussion on this question might benefit from first describing just what a strict teacher is. Some characteristics of strict teachers are providing challenging work, expecting students to do all assignments on time, and handing out good grades only for good work.

4. *Besides the threat of failure, what are some other ways that teachers can motivate students? What have teachers done to make you want to work harder for a class?*

   Answers will vary. As Sherry implies in paragraph 4, a teacher's style is one important factor in gaining students' attention and getting them to work harder. The more interested a student is in a class, the harder he or she will probably work. Other ideas teachers have used include providing rewards for good work, such as praise and awards; bringing people with interesting careers into class to inform and motivate students; and using reading materials that are relevant to students' lives.

10 GAMBLING—A DANGEROUS GAME, Jon Volkmer

1. Do you think Jon Volkmer did the right thing by helping Tom get home from Las Vegas? Why or why not?

Students who think Volkmer did the right thing might say that it would have been inhumane to not help Tom, who was clearly desperate. To have refused to help Tom get home would have only added to Tom's problems. Students who disagree with Volkmer's decision might say that Tom needed to "hit bottom" before he got serious about solving his gambling problem, and that helping Tom get home from Las Vegas might have enabled him to sweep the problem under the rug for another period.

2. Volkmer proposes several possible reasons why people find gambling attractive. Do you know anyone with a gambling problem? Why do you think this person (or people in general) cannot resist gambling?

Answers will vary. In general, though, gambling is attractive because of the prospect of easy money and the adrenaline rush of taking risks. As people fall more into debt , the need for a big win increases and encourages them to gamble even more recklessly.

3. If it were up to you, would you put more legal restrictions on gambling, or would you relax the legal restrictions on gambling? Explain.

Answers will vary.

4. Tom says he thinks those who profit from gambling, such as the government and casinos, should "spend a lot more in outreach, education and treatment for those addicted to gambling." Do you agree? Should the government and casinos share responsibility for the gamblers' addiction?

Students will probably divide into two camps on this question. One will believe that the entities that profit from people's love of gambling are cruelly exploiting people's weaknesses and should help out-of-control gamblers get help. Others will say that people need to take personal responsibility for their self-destructive choices, whether those choices be gambling, smoking, drinking, or overeating.

SUGGESTED ANSWERS TO THE DISCUSSION QUESTIONS IN PART TWO

Note: The numbers in parentheses refer to paragraphs in the reading. For some questions, additional related questions have been included to enhance class discussion.

1   THE YELLOW RIBBON, Pete Hamill

1. According to the information in the selection, what is Vingo's attitude toward his wife?

Vingo clearly loves his wife and hopes that she will take him back, although he has left the decision up to her and expects the worst (17–19). While in prison, he wrote to her, "I understand if you can't stay married to me." He even suggested the possibility that she'd find "a new guy—she's a wonderful woman, really something" (17). He has told her not to write to him and has even spared her the possible pain of seeing him again: if she doesn't want him back, all she has to do is *not* tie the yellow handkerchief to the tree (19). He shows "a cracked, much-handled snapshot" of his wife and family to the young people (21)—further evidence of his love.

What might his wife's feelings have been upon learning her husband had to go to prison? Why might she not have written to him for three and a half years?

2. Has Vingo assumed responsibility for his crime, in your opinion?

Answers will vary, but they should take into consideration the fact that Vingo said, "I did it and I went to jail. If you can't do the time, don't do the crime" (13).

3. While there is much we don't learn about Vingo in this very short narrative, Hamill does provide us with clues to some important aspects of his personality. What evidence is there that he is a decent man, a person who we could feel deserves a second chance?

• Vingo's "cocoon of silence" (2) suggests that he sometimes dealt with important issues very introspectively. He does not seem afraid of coming to terms with his feelings.

• He is willing to take responsibility for himself and others. He took responsibility for his actions by accepting the idea that he earned imprisonment: "I did it and I went to jail. If you can't do the time, don't do the crime" (13). This also suggests that Vingo took some responsibility in making a point of showing young people the hazards of crime.

• He was probably ashamed of what he did and did not expect his wife to be loyal to him any more (17–19). This shows, again, his understanding of his errors and willingness to own up to them.

• When it came to his family, he was appreciative and loving (17–21). He is also unselfish in freeing his wife from any responsibility towards him while he is in prison and even suggesting she find "a new guy" (17). His words to her reveal that he places her feelings and needs ahead of his.

• He has a personality that attracted the young people to him and made them—and his wife!—care about him (21).

4. *Many people are thrilled, some even to tears, by this story. What makes "The Yellow Ribbon" have such a powerful effect on readers?*

Like the young people, the reader begins to care a lot about Vingo and his fate. He is at a turning point in his life, and what happens at the tree means a great deal in terms of both his past and his future. We all can empathize with anticipation of such moments. Hamill accents the drama of that moment by building up to it and saving it for last. This moment is especially meaningful because it represents that which we all seek—unconditional love. We all want to have someone ready to fill up a tree with ribbons of acceptance of us and to take us back into his or her life, no matter what mistakes we have made. We all want forgiveness and the right to a second chance.

2 THE CERTAINTY OF FEAR, Audra Kendall

1. *Did you, like the author, have a beloved toy or doll when you were a small child? Why was it so special to you? How would you have responded if you had lost it?*

Answers will vary.

2. *What do you think of psychologist David Elkind's "Imaginary Audience Theory" of adolescence? Did you feel the kind of self-consciousness he describes when you were an adolescent? Do you observe that kind of behavior in other teens?*

Answers will vary.

3. *Have you observed someone going through what seemed to be a midlife crisis? What behaviors did you notice?*

Answers will vary.

4. *The author writes, "And that, I think, is the essence of fear—the threat of loss." Do you agree with her? What are some examples you can think of in which fears are caused by the threat of loss?*

Answers will vary.

3 SHAME, Dick Gregory

1. *Why did Gregory include both the classroom and the restaurant anecdotes in one selection? What is the difference between the shame he felt in the first incident and the shame he felt in the second? What are the similarities between the two incidents?*

Had "Shame" not included the anecdote abut the wino, it would have focused on only one type of shame, that shame people feel when others look down on them (5, 6), ignore their feelings (16–22), and feel sorry for them (28, sentence 2). The story about the wino introduces another type of shame. This type of shame—which Gregory felt when he "waited too long to help another man"—results when someone makes another person feel the first type of shame.

The similarity between the two incidents is that in both cases someone has not taken another unfortunate person's feelings into account. In the first anecdote, Gregory is on the receiving end of inconsiderate behavior. In the second, he is the inconsiderate one. He seems to be saying that the shame he felt in the second case was much greater.

2. *The Community Chest incident could have had very different results if Gregory's teacher had handled the situation in another way. What do you think she should have done when Gregory said, "You forgot me"?*

Answers will vary. A more compassionate response on the teacher's part would have been to realize Gregory's need to be included and to go along with his pretense. Instead of embarrassing him in front of the entire class, the teacher could have asked Gregory to see her after class alone to talk about why he needed to "buy a Daddy."

3. *One type of irony is an event or an effect that is the opposite of what might be expected. In what ways are the following parts of "Shame" ironic?*

- *I never learned hate at home, or shame. I had to go to school for that.*

    The irony here is that school is meant to teach us something better than shame.

- *If I knew my place and didn't come too close, she'd wink at me and say hello. That was a good feeling.*

    We might not expect someone to feel good about knowing his "place" and keeping his distance.

- *I looked at the wino with blood all over his face and I went over. "Leave him alone, Mister Williams. I'll pay the twenty-six cents."*
    The wino got up . . . . He looked at me with pure hate.

    We would not expect a response that seems to be generous to be met with "pure hate."

    In each of these cases, Gregory makes us think twice about how people make each other feel. In so doing, he enriches our understanding of his descriptions of shame.

4. *Has anyone ever tried to help you in a way that didn't take all your needs into account? If so, how did you feel toward that person? In what ways might activities that are meant to help people also hurt them?*

Answers will vary. Possible avenues of discussion include ways our social agencies help people, how family members help and hurt each other, and how schools sometimes teach negative lessons instead of positive ones.

1. Have you ever been in a situation where the bystander effect played a part? Would your behavior be any different in light of what you have learned from this article?

Answers will vary.

2. The author states in paragraph 31, "Bystanders look to others for cues as to what is happening. Frequently other witnesses, just as confused, try to look calm." Why do you think witnesses would try to look calm during an emergency?

Answers will vary. A possible clue is in paragraph 29: "Bystanders are afraid to endanger themselves or look foolish if they take the wrong action in a situation they're not sure how to interpret." Rather than reveal their fear or confusion, they might mask it with pretense: I'm in control; I know what's really going on; this isn't as bad as it looks (and therefore doesn't warrant my interference).

3. In paragraph 33, the author suggests that if you understand what causes "the bystander effect," you can act appropriately in an emergency: "If you take action, others may also help." If, say, you were in a group of onlookers while a fight was in progress, what could you do that would encourage others to intervene?

The article implies that whatever you do to weaken the level of ambiguity will encourage bystander intervention (29). Thus any action that can be readily interpreted by others to mean they are not in danger and will not look foolish would be encouraging. Perhaps such actions will also remind bystanders that group morality (32) tends to be influenced by individual actions.

4. How does the conclusion of this article clarify the author's purpose for the reader? How does the article's beginning fit in with that purpose?

Paragraphs 2–32 present only the facts about the bystander effect. Thus without its beginning and conclusion, the article would appear to be written simply to inform the reader. By raising the issue of the reader's "appropriate action" (33), however, the ending reveals the author's persuasive purpose—to convince readers to overcome the bystander effect. The beginning of the article also points to that purpose by raising the question of how readers, rather than hypothetical people, would respond in certain emergency situations.

"LET'S ROLL." Karen Breslau, Eleanor Clift, and Evan Thomas

1. *Where were you on the terrible day of September 11th, 2001, and what were your reactions to the events of that day?*

   Answers will vary.

2. *How did reading this selection affect you? For example, as you were reading, did you feel pity, anger, horror, surprise, admiration, pride, or a combination of the above? Explain.*

   Answers will vary, but most students will react to the selection with a combination of emotions.

3. *While the selection focuses mainly on the struggle between a group of passengers and the hijackers, we are also given specific details about individual passengers. Which details would you say are particularly effective in making you see these people as individuals? If you could interview any of the passengers, whom would you choose, and what questions would you want to ask?*

   Students will probably mention the personal details about individual passengers in paragraph 17, revealing these passengers' physical strength and ability to cope with crisis or danger, and the quoted excerpts from telephone calls, which attest to the passengers' courage and selflessness. Answers to the second question will vary.

6   COPING WITH NERVOUSNESS, Rudolph F. Verderber

1. What have your public speaking experiences been like? Have some speeches gone better than others? If so, what were the differences, and what do you think were the reasons for those differences? What did you find helpful in preparing and giving speeches?

Answers will vary.

2. Why might it be a good idea to speak on a topic you know a great deal about and are interested in? Can you think of any examples from the speeches you've given or heard?

Verderber writes, "If you feel in command of your material . . . , you'll be far more confident" (9). A speaker will certainly be in command of material when the topic is one that he or she knows a great deal about. With such a topic, a speaker isn't just memorizing facts and ideas; he or she is putting into words ideas that are very familiar.

3. You may need to give speeches in your classes, but do you think you will have to speak in public after you graduate from school? In what situations might you have to give a speech or even a presentation to a small group?

People in such fields as politics and religion may routinely have to give speeches, but people in a variety of other arenas also must speak before groups. Following are some examples:

- A company manager presents new information to the ten people in his or her department
- A Sunday school instructor teaches a lesson to thirty students
- A volunteer gives a report at a meeting attended by fifty others
- A firefighter explains safety rules to an auditorium full of students
- A salesperson reports on his or her department at a company meeting

4. Obviously, Verderber feels that nervousness is no reason to avoid speaking in public. What other activities have you willingly done despite the fact that they made you nervous in some way? Was being nervous in these situations helpful in some ways? If so, how?

Answers will vary. Following are some other activities that people do for various reasons despite the fact that they make them nervous:

- Asking someone out on a date
- Going for a job interview
- Taking the writing and driving tests for a driver's license
- Getting married in front of a crowd of family and friends

7   COMPLIANCE TECHNIQUES, Shelley E. Taylor, Letitia Anne Peplau, and David O. Sears

1. *While reading this selection, did you recognize techniques that have been used to influence you to make a purchase or support someone's plan? How were the techniques used?*

Answers will vary. Situations in which such techniques are commonly used include calls from charitable organizations, sales calls, sales ads, bargaining, and in-store pricing.

2. *Which of the compliance techniques do you feel is most clearly deceptive? Why?*

Answers will vary, but the only technique pointed out by the authors as being clearly deceptive is the low-ball technique, about which they write:

> Essentially, the person is tricked into agreeing to a relatively attractive proposition, only to discover later that the terms are actually different from those expected. . . . Although this technique can be effective . . . , it is clearly deceptive . . . laws have been enacted to make low-balling illegal for several industries. (11)

3. *The authors state that no one is really sure why the "foot-in-the-door" technique is effective, but they offer two possible explanations. Does either of those explanations seem to you to adequately explain why the technique works? Can you think of an alternative explanation?*

Answers will vary. A possible third explanation may be that people feel refusing the second request will appear to be backing off from their original commitment, something they are embarrassed to do.

4. *Imagine that you are in the business of selling home computers. Describe how you would use the foot-in-the-door technique, the door-in-the-face technique, and the low-ball technique to try to make a sale.*

A *foot-in-the-door technique* to sell home computers might be to ask customers to rent a computer for a short time. Once a customer views himself or herself as a computer user, he or she might be more willing to buy. A *door-in-the-face technique* to sell home computers might involve asking a customer to buy the top-of-the-line computer and then offering something notably less expensive. In a *low-ball technique* to sell home computers, the customer might at first be told only the price of the computer itself. Once the customer shows interest, then the salesperson would add on the prices of necessary adjuncts to the computer—the software and the printer.

8   LIZZIE BORDEN, James Kirby Martin and others

1.   On the basis of the information in the reading, do you agree or disagree with the experts who say Lizzie was guilty? Explain your answer.

Answers will vary.

2.   As you read this selection, what impression did you form of life in the Borden household? What particular details helped you form that opinion?

In paragraph 2, the authors provide various details to show how for Lizzie (and Emma) "life in the flats was an intolerable embarrassment" and grim. Furthermore, the authors show that Lizzie's parents themselves added to the discomfort of the household: In paragraphs 1 and 2, Andrew is depicted as ungenerous and unamusing, and in paragraph 2 we are told that Lizzie "strongly disliked" her stepmother.

3.   The authors imply that the story about Andrew Borden's cutting off the feet of corpses to make them fit undersized coffins was a rumor, not a proved fact. Why, then, do you think they include the story in this piece?

The story is a colorful, dramatic example of Borden's reputation. Even if the story isn't true, the details of the selection suggest that the character implications behind the story are true.

4.   Do you believe that any of the notions about women that existed in Lizzie Borden's day are still at work in some ways today? Explain your answer.

Following are the notions about women mentioned in the selection:

- "Society expected a woman of social position to marry, and while she waited for a proper suitor, her only respectable social outlets were church and community service" (3).

- "A woman of Lizzie's social position, they affirmed, simply could not have committed such a terrible crime" (7).

- " 'Americans were certain that well-brought up daughters could not commit murder with a hatchet on sunny summer mornings.' Criminal women, they believed, originated in the lower classes and even looked evil" (8).

- "Jurors and editorialists alike judged Lizzie according to their preconceived notions of Victorian womanhood. They believed that such a woman was gentle, docile, and physically frail, short on analytical ability but long on nurturing instincts" (9).

- " 'Women,' wrote an editorialist for *Scribner's*, 'are merely large babies. They are shortsighted, frivolous, and occupy an intermediate stage between children and men' " (9).

- "Too uncoordinated and weak to accurately swing an ax and too gentle and unintelligent to coldly plan a double murder, women of Lizzie's background simply had to be innocent because of their basic innocence" (9).

To what extent are any of the above points of view still at work today? What examples of women are there in American society today—and in other countries—that contradict the above views?

1. What are your answers to the following questions from the selection? Why do you think the author included these questions?

- *Why do you think we allow a doctor to easily violate our intimate distance zone?*

We give the goal of maintaining and improving our health priority over other considerations. The question, however, is a reminder that despite that goal, many of us are still uncomfortable when the doctor does "violate our intimate distance zone." Like the following two questions, this question underlines the intensity of our feelings about those zones.

- *I can remember becoming angry and generally irritated when a friend of mine placed a plate and glass in my space. . . . Has this ever happened to you?*

Students may think of similar situations, such as someone sitting closer to them than the distance other people were sitting from each other at a table.

- *What would violate the social distance norms in a classroom?*

Such violations might include a girl sitting on her boyfriend's lap, the teacher discussing his or her personal problems in class, and somebody knitting during a lecture.

2. This selection includes headings, italics, labels, and numbered items. How are these related to the author's purpose?

The author's purpose is to inform. By helping readers to be aware of the article's enumerations and organization, he is helping them to understand and remember the information he presents.
   How does this structure relate to the benefits of outlining a reading?

3. What are some examples of a dating or business situation in which someone's body language might contradict his or her verbal communication?

Grasha explains that "we have less conscious control over the specific body gestures or expressions we might make while talking." Thus whenever we say one thing and mean another, our body language is likely to contradict what we say. There are therefore many possible answers to this question, including the following:

- In a conversation with someone at a party, we might appear to be listening and responding, but our eyes may be looking around the room for a more interesting person to talk to.
- During a job evaluation, we might be saying "yes" to our supervisor's suggestions for changes, but our arms might be crossed and our jaw clenched, indicating we do not agree with his or her recommendations.

   What other postures, facial expressions, hand and arm movements might give away the fact that a person is saying one thing but means another?

4. Give examples from your own experience of all four types of personal space.

Answers will vary.

1. *In the course of your education, have you met any students like Gerald—or have you ever had a bit of Gerald in yourself? What do you think people like Gerald have to do to take charge of their lives?*

Answers will vary, but one thought students might consider is that people are most comfortable with what they are accustomed to. If they have gotten used to defeat and failure, they may act in ways that guarantee further failure (such as not showing up for class) rather than risking new, unfamiliar behaviors. They may need to ask themselves why they choose failure over success before taking steps to change their behaviors.

2. *What escape routes are you most likely to use to avoid studying? What can you do to avoid them?*

Answers will vary.

3. *Describe someone you know (it could be you) who has a dream—and who is the better off for it. Also describe someone you know who does* not *have a dream. Do you agree or disagree that it's important to have a dream?*

Answers will vary.

4. *In "The Power Within," the author quotes such inspirational figures as Mahatma Gandhi, Robert Kennedy, Dr. Martin Luther King, and Oprah Winfrey. Who inspires you? Why?*

Answers will vary.

TEST BANK

This section contains the following:

- A **Test Bank** (pages 45–132) consisting of four additional mastery tests for each chapter in Part One of *Ten Steps to Improving College Reading Skills*, Fifth Edition, as well as four additional Combined-Skills Mastery Tests;
- An **answer key** (pages 133–136) to the 44 tests in the test bank.

Instructors whose students are using *Ten Steps to Improving College Reading Skills*, Fifth Edition, in class have permission to reproduce any of these tests on a photocopying machine (or a secure website) as often as needed.

VOCABULARY IN CONTEXT: Test A

A. For each item below, underline the **examples** that suggest the meaning of the italicized term. Then, in the space provided, write the letter of the meaning of that term.

___ 1. Most daydreams concern such *mundane* events as paying the telephone bill and picking up the groceries.
    A. complicated   C. proper
    B. ordinary   D. exciting

___ 2. Everyone has their *foibles,* and I admit that mine include eating with my hands and being late everywhere I go.
    A. strengths   C. hobbies
    B. minor faults   D. crimes

___ 3. The supervisor's day was filled with one minor *calamity* after another. In the morning, his car broke down; at lunchtime, he lost his wallet; and at the end of the day, his computer crashed and he lost a day's work.
    A. requirement   C. question
    B. claim   D. disaster

B. Each item below includes a word or words that are a **synonym** of the italicized word. Write the synonym of the italicized word in the space provided.

_____ 4. You can't do algebra until you have mastered *rudimentary* math skills—basic addition, subtraction, multiplication, and division.

_____ 5. Love is not always considered a *prerequisite* for marriage. In some cultures, social status or economic potential is a more important requirement.

_____ 6. According to recent studies, a shortage of sleep due to long work or study hours will not cause any permanent damage to your health. One good night of sleep, researchers say, can make up for a week of sleep *deficit.*

C. Each item below includes a word or words that are an **antonym** of the italicized word. Underline the antonym of each italicized word. Then write the letter of the meaning of the italicized word.

___ 7. The children wanted us to adopt an older German shepherd from the pound, but we were told he was rather wild, so instead we chose a collie that was more *docile.*
    A. manageable   C. expensive
    B. disobedient   D. temporary

(Continues on next page)

_____ 8. Though the United States is one of the most *affluent* nations in the world, one in four children grow up in poor circumstances.
    A. famous   C. wealthy
    B. active   D. large

D. Use the **general sense of each sentence** to figure out the meaning of each italicized word. Then write the letter of the meaning of the italicized word.

_____ 9. The journalism instructor *denounced* local news shows for emphasizing crime, fires, and the like at the expense of more important city issues.
    A. stopped   C. admired
    B. joined   D. criticized

_____10. After a hundred years of its "boys only" policy, a military school finally decided to *deviate* from its tradition and let females in.
    A. depart   C. learn
    B. borrow   D. accept

VOCABULARY IN CONTEXT: Test B

A. For each item below, underline the **examples** that suggest the meaning of the italicized term. Then, in the space provided, write the letter of the meaning of that term.

___ 1. I'm happy sightseeing *vicariously,* for instance, by watching travel TV shows and visiting faraway places on the Internet.
   A. personally
   B. expensively
   C. indirectly
   D. energetically

___ 2. There are good reasons to think TV has a *detrimental* influence on kids. After all, TV watching keeps them from exercising, encourages them to eat unhealthy foods, and teaches them to be violent.
   A. deadly
   B. dull
   C. strong
   D. harmful

B. Each item below includes a word or words that are a **synonym** of the italicized word. Write the synonym of the italicized word in the space provided.

_____ 3. New inventions make old ones *obsolete.* For instance, because of the compact disk, the phonograph record is now outdated.

_____ 4. During the fourteenth century, the Black Death *decimated* one third of the population of Europe. Two centuries later, smallpox wiped out 95 percent of the native population of Mexico.

_____ 5. Until recently, immunization seemed to have erased the *peril* of diseases such as measles, rubella, and mumps, but now the threat of these dangerous illnesses is growing.

C. Each item below includes a word or words that are an **antonym** of the italicized word. Underline the antonym of each italicized word. Then write the letter of the meaning of the italicized word.

___ 6. To a person sitting by the shore of a peaceful lake, the environment seems silent. But to the sensitive ears of a dog, the same area may be a *clamorous* place filled with the buzzing of insects and the bustling of small animals.
   A. natural
   B. noisy
   C. boring
   D. dangerous

(Continues on next page)

___ 7. Some scientists think dreams express hidden wishes and desires. Others disagree, arguing instead that dreams deal with more *overt* concerns, such as the people and problems in our everyday lives.
   A. obvious   C. damaging
   B. informal   D. mysterious

___ 8. While the passion of love may *wane* over time, intimacy tends to grow. This change often results in a more rewarding connection than the emotional roller coaster that is often the case in the early stages of relationships.
   A. frighten   C. lessen
   B. expand   D. transfer

D. Use the **general sense of each sentence** to figure out the meaning of each italicized word. Then write the letter of the meaning of the italicized word.

___ 9. Watching television is, above all, a *passive* experience. One sits back and waits to be entertained.
   A. complicated   C. aggressive
   B. expensive   D. inactive

___10. Today many young couples are *ambivalent* about having children; they cannot decide which is more important—pursuing their careers or building a family.
   A. knowledgeable   C. sure
   B. having mixed feelings   D. tired

VOCABULARY IN CONTEXT: Test C

Using context clues for help, write the letter of the best meaning for each italicized word or words.

____ 1. Grasshoppers are a prized food in some places, but most people in Western societies find them *repugnant*.
   A. delightful   C. confusing
   B. disgusting   D. filling

____ 2. My brother's irresponsible work habits are gradually *eroding* his boss's confidence in him.
   A. equal to   C. wearing away
   B. building   D. preserving

____ 3. I want to teach my children to be *wary* of strangers without making them overly fearful of people they don't know.
   A. neighborly   C. unsuspecting
   B. careful   D. surprised

____ 4. Even while in the womb, a baby can *discriminate* between the voice of its mother and that of another woman.
   A. be confused   C. distinguish
   B. cry   D. play

____ 5. After winning the basketball championship, the players *flaunted* their victory by screaming over and over, "We won!"
   A. lied about   C. forgot
   B. exaggerated   D. showed off

____ 6. People who experience too much stress are *prone* to such health problems as flu, sore throat, headaches, and backaches.
   A. likely to have   C. responding
   B. protected   D. too busy for

____ 7. The time we spend dreaming *dwindles* over our lifetimes. Babies dream as much as eight hours a day, but adults dream less than two hours each night.
   A. passes   C. connects
   B. shrinks   D. adds up

____ 8. A generation or two ago, it was considered rude to bring up three topics in polite conversation: politics, religion, and sex. Nowadays, however, we do not *adhere to* such limitations.
   A. change   C. follow
   B. mind   D. question

(Continues on next page)

___ 9. When speaking to a large audience, it is helpful to remember that people are *egocentric*. They pay closest attention to messages about their own values, their own beliefs, and their own well-being.

    A. self-centered   C. understanding

    B. impatient   D. self-controlled

___10. The chapter ended with the hero in the *precarious* position of hanging from a cliff.

    A. unimportant   C. cautious

    B. ordinary   D. dangerous

VOCABULARY IN CONTEXT: Test D

Using context clues for help, write the letter of the best meaning for each italicized word or words.

____ 1. Open communication can lead to healthier relationships. Research shows that couples who often *disclose* their feelings to each other report having stronger feelings of love and happiness than others.
   A. change   C. reveal
   B. forget   D. foresee

____ 2. In a political cartoon, the senator was *depicted* as a baseball player who struck out.
   A. photographed   C. joined
   B. represented   D. quoted

____ 3. There is still a great *discrepancy* between the wages the sexes earn. For every dollar that men make, women earn only seventy cents.
   A. similarity   C. advantage
   B. logic   D. difference

____ 4. In addition to working full-time at the bank, Emilio *augments* his income during the holiday season by working several nights a week at a local department store.
   A. replaces   C. overlooks
   B. saves   D. adds to

____ 5. In intense summer heat and humidity, I feel so *lackadaisical* that all I want to do is sleep, eat, and then sleep some more.
   A. angry   C. lazy
   B. well-off   D. ill

____ 6. The manager said not only is it *feasible* to repair the tire instead of replacing it, but it is also possible to have it done by tonight.
   A. achievable   C. late
   B. unreasonable   D. early

____ 7. In the 1950s, the nation's *flourishing* economy provided middle-class people with the money they needed to buy new homes outside of overcrowded urban areas. Thus the movement from the cities to the suburbs grew.
   A. failing   C. farm
   B. successful   D. dried-up

____ 8. Jimmy made several *overtures* to the new boy next door, including inviting him to a barbecue and asking him to play with his friends.
   A. invitations   C. excuses
   B. remarks   D. jokes

(Continues on next page)

___ 9. Scientists find that when people feel "love at first sight," the pleasure center of the brain releases a chemical that *stimulates* the body, causing rapid heartbeat, giddiness, and deep breathing.

A. makes more active   C. bypasses

B. quiets down   D. imitates

___10. In ancient Greece, love had been regarded as somewhat undesirable, a divine punishment. By the twelfth century, poets in Europe had taken this *notion* even further; love, they argued, was a sweet form of suffering.

A. reason   C. hope

B. punishment   D. idea

Name _____

Section _____ Date _____

SCORE: (Number correct) × 20 = _____%

MAIN IDEAS: Test A

The following selections have main ideas that may appear at any place within the paragraph. Identify the main idea of each paragraph by filling in the correct sentence number in the space provided.

___ 1. ¹Often when older children move back home, unpleasant tensions and disagreements arise. ²However, adult children who move back home can avoid family conflicts by following some tips. ³First, they should contribute what they can—and it need not be in terms of money: Being productive family members will help them earn their keep. ⁴This can involve tutoring or coaching younger sisters or brothers, or helping Mom and Dad with chores and errands. ⁵Second, these "returnees" should not expect their parents to rescue them from difficulties. ⁶As adults, they are responsible for getting out of their own scrapes—and for trying to avoid them in the first place. ⁷Last, they must respect their parents' lifestyles and own needs for independence. ⁸It is unrealistic to expect parents' lives to revolve around the needs of a grown child, in the manner they may have when the child was younger.

___ 2. ¹Scientists have learned that the way we view exercise strongly influences our performance. ²Research on Russian weight lifters, for example, demonstrated that if they were told the weights were heavy, they perceived an exercise to be more difficult. ³If they were told the weights were light, then they considered the exercise easier. ⁴Another example is the weight lifter who kept failing to break a record. ⁵He finally succeeded after his trainer told him the weights he was lifting were not as heavy as they in fact were.

___ 3. ¹Until the 1940s, most Americans were born and died at home. ²Births and deaths happened when they happened, often without medical intervention. ³If a baby was too premature or defective, or if a seriously ill person was dying, there was little the family doctor could do about it other than to offer comfort. ⁴Today, most Americans are born and die in hospitals under the supervision of medical personnel who sometimes decide to keep them alive long beyond the point at which they would normally have died. ⁵Patients can be hooked up for days, months, or years to machines that sustain their lives. ⁶This step may be taken even if they are in constant pain or permanently comatose. ⁷Obviously, technology has greatly changed how we are born and die.

(Continues on next page)

____ 4. [1]Though natural-fiber purists may turn up their noses at it, polyester-and-cotton-blend clothing has advantages over all-cotton garments. [2]For one thing, polyester, which is manufactured, costs less than cotton, which grows naturally but is expensive to process. [3]Therefore, cotton/polyester clothing is more economical than pure cotton garments. [4]Also, the polyester content of cotton-blend clothing helps the garments retain their shape after repeated washings. [5]That's because this synthetic does not share cotton's tendency to shrink or stretch after immersion. [6]But perhaps polyester's most endearing quality is its "no-wrinkle policy." [7]Unlike pure cotton, polyester blends require little or no ironing!

____ 5. [1]Baseball enthusiasts hold softball in low esteem. [2]It's a picnic game, they argue, with a big, soft ball, shorter base paths, and a pitcher who throws underhand. [3]Yet fast-pitch softball can be as intense and dramatic as any baseball game—perhaps more so. [4]True, the base paths are shorter, but ask any third baseman how quickly a well-hit groundball reaches him on softball's smaller diamond. [5]True, the pitcher throws underhand, but he stands fifteen feet closer to the plate, and he might hit speeds exceeding eighty miles per hour. [6]True, the ball is softer than a baseball, but catch a hard one in the ribs just once, and such knowledge is small comfort.

MAIN IDEAS: Test B

The following selections have main ideas that may appear at any place within the paragraph. Identify the main idea of each paragraph by filling in the correct sentence number in the space provided.

____ 1. ¹Plastic trash bags were once considered a major menace to the environment. ²The makers of plastic trash bags responded to the environmental concerns and made several positive changes in their product. ³First, they made use of a new additive—actually, potato peels—to make the bags biodegradable (that is, capable of breaking down and being absorbed by the environment). ⁴Next, they removed any ingredients in their plastic formula which would contaminate soil in a landfill. ⁵Finally, they made it possible for the bags to be burned safely, without adding dangerous pollutants to the air.

____ 2. ¹Snoring is the number-one complaint in marriages all around the world. ²The honks, hoots, and snorts created by snorers annoy their mates and deprive them of sleep. ³Fortunately, there are some means of preventing snoring. ⁴First, the snorer should avoid breathing through his mouth. ⁵Mouth-breathing can be discouraged if the snorer sleeps on his side with his forearm under his chin—effectively pressing his mouth shut. ⁶Second, the snorer should increase the humidity in his bedroom. ⁷A humidifier or even a pot of water in the room may help. ⁸In addition, snoring may disappear if an overweight snorer loses some pounds. ⁹And finally, a snorer should avoid drinking alcohol in the evening.

____ 3. ¹A young girl looks at a fashion magazine and sees clothes modeled by women carrying 115 pounds on their five-foot-ten-inch frames. ²She receives a "teen doll" as a present and studies its proportions: legs nearly two-thirds the length of its body, tiny waist, non-existent hips and thighs. ³She goes to the movies and observes screen heroines who in their leanness resemble adolescent boys more than mature women. ⁴Her favorite television shows are filled with commercials for weight-loss programs that equate slenderness with desirability. ⁵By the time the girl reaches her teens, she has been thoroughly bombarded with society's message that to be thin is the only acceptable option.

(Continues on next page)

___ 4. [1]Symbols can have a tremendously powerful emotional impact upon us, instantly conveying many feelings and ideas. [2]Symbols like the cross, the Star of David, or the star-and-crescent immediately make us think of the Christian, Jewish, or Muslim religions. [3]This may be why burning an American flag often arouses more anger than does an attack on the values for which the flag actually stands. [4]Another symbol with terrible power is the swastika. [5]Until this century, the swastika was an innocent traditional symbol found in many cultures. [6]Then it became the symbol of Nazi terror. [7]Today, the very sight of a swastika can send chills down our spines.

___ 5. [1]Can psychics see into the future? [2]Although one might wish for a psychic stock forecaster, the tallied forecasts of "leading psychics" reveal little accuracy. [3]In one eight-year period, the New Year's predictions of the *National Enquirer*'s favorite psychics yielded two accurate predictions out of 486. [4]During the early 1990s, tabloid psychics were all wrong in predicting surprising events (Madonna did not become a gospel singer, a UFO base was not found in the Mexican desert, Queen Elizabeth did not abdicate her throne to enter a convent). [5]And they missed all the significant unexpected events, such as the breakup of the Soviet Union, Saddam Hussein's assault on Kuwait, and the O.J. Simpson case. [6]Before 1994, psychics offered many predictions about Michael Jackson—that he would marry Oprah Winfrey, become a traveling evangelist, and have a sex-change operation—but missed their chance to predict his marriage to Lisa Marie Presley.

MAIN IDEAS: Test C

The following selections have main ideas that may appear at any place within the paragraph. Identify the main idea of each paragraph by filling in the correct sentence number in the space provided.

____ 1. [1]For many years, there has been a section in *Reader's Digest* magazine called "Laughter, the Best Medicine." [2]The name is not an exaggeration—medical studies show that laughter is good for one's physical and emotional health. [3]A hearty laugh exercises the internal organs, including the heart and lungs. [4]The deep breathing that accompanies laughter supplies your body with extra oxygen. [5]Many diseases deplete the body's supply of oxygen, so getting extra oxygen is important. [6]Laughter may also stimulate the body's production of endorphins, which act as painkillers and antidepressants.

____ 2. [1]Scientists predict that textbooks of the future will be computerized and will thus offer many of the special benefits unique to computers. [2]First of all, they say that the books will take the form of small plastic cards that can be inserted into screens the size of paperback novels. [3]Viewers will be able to select the size and style of print and automatic page turning, or they may choose to listen to an audio version and just watch the pictures. [4]They will be able to zoom in for close-ups of illustrations, which will then fill the screen and rotate for a three-dimensional view, so that medical students, for example, can see all sides of a muscle and how it moves. [5]Finally, viewers will be able to interact with materials by typing in critical comments, updating information, and even changing the outcome of a story.

____ 3. [1]A major study of firstborn children reveals that they tend to be super-achievers who strive very hard to make their families proud. [2]It was discovered that of the country's first twenty-three astronauts, an amazing twenty-one were firstborn in their families. [3]Also, slightly more than half—52 percent—of our presidents were firstborn children. [4]Less positive is the fact that firstborns are under a lot of pressure to succeed, because their families often pin their hopes and dreams on them. [5]Also, as the eldest, they are expected to "set an example" for their younger brothers and sisters. [6]Furthermore, these firstborns sometimes have trouble with personal relationships because they learned to be very independent and to enjoy doing things on their own—since they were the only children in their families until their younger brothers and sisters were born. [7]The conclusion of the study is that being a firstborn child is a mixed blessing, having positive as well as some negative aspects.

(Continues on next page)

___ 4. ¹Unlike many lower animals that use their noses to detect mates, predators, and prey, humans do not depend on their sense of smell for survival. ²Nevertheless, the sense of smell in humans is incredibly sensitive. ³Only a few molecules of a substance reaching the smell receptors are necessary to cause humans to perceive an odor. ⁴Certain substances can be detected in especially small amounts. ⁵Decayed cabbage, lemons, and rotten eggs are examples. ⁶So too is mercaptan, a foul-smelling substance added to natural gas that we can smell in concentrations as small as one part per fifty billion parts of air. ⁷According to one estimate, the sense of smell is about ten thousand times more sensitive than that of taste.

___ 5. ¹At the outset of the nineteenth century, there was a lack of reliable, comfortable travel. ²The stagecoach was the major form of transportation. ³Twelve passengers, crowded along with their bags and parcels, traveled at just four miles an hour. ⁴Wretched roads plagued travelers. ⁵Larger towns had roads paved with cobblestones; potholes in major highways were filled with stones. ⁶Most roads were simply dirt paths. ⁷Rain left these roads muddy and rutted. ⁸The presence of tree stumps in the middle of many roads posed a serious obstacle to carriages.

MAIN IDEAS: Test D

The following selections have main ideas that may appear at any place within the paragraph. Identify the main idea of each paragraph by filling in the correct sentence number in the space provided.

____ 1. ¹The personalities of adopted children do not much resemble those of their adoptive parents. ²Studies show, however, that adoptive parents do have many generally positive effects on their children. ³First, the home environment influences adopted children's values, beliefs, and social attitudes. ⁴Second, in adoptive homes, child neglect and abuse are rare. ⁵Adopted children are less than half as likely as other children to have divorced or separated parents. ⁶Adoptive parents are carefully screened; natural parents are not. ⁷So it is not surprising that nearly all adopted children thrive. ⁸They score higher than their biological parents on intelligence tests, and many become happier and more stable people than they would have in a stressed or neglectful environment.

____ 2. ¹Self-serving bonds exist between unrelated members of the animal kingdom. ²Take the leopard and the battler eagle, for instance. ³A leopard will go to any lengths to keep other animals from its kill, even to the point of storing the carcass high above the ground in the fork of a tree. ⁴But the leopard enters into a firm partnership with the battler eagle who, in return for a share of the meat, guards the kill and warns the leopard about potential poachers. ⁵Or consider the rhinoceros and its flocks of tickbirds and egrets. ⁶The rhino, nearly blind, relies on the birds' eyesight to warn it of approaching danger, while the birds fill themselves up on the host of ticks and other parasites infecting the rhino's hide. ⁷Even in the ocean, these beneficial relationships flourish. ⁸Moray eels and cleaner fish, for example, peacefully inhabit the same reef. ⁹The cleaner fish get an all-you-can-eat dinner on the eel's parasites, and the eel receives a free grooming session.

____ 3. ¹Imagine a successful fisherman who needs a new sail for his boat. ²In a barter economy—that is, one in which goods are exchanged directly for one another—he would have to find someone who not only needs fish but is willing to exchange a sail for it. ³If no sailmaker wants fish, the fisherman must find someone else—say, a shoemaker—who wants fish and will trade for it. ⁴The fisherman must hope that the sailmaker will trade for the shoes. ⁵In a money economy, the fisherman would sell his catch, receive money, and exchange the money for such goods as a new sail. ⁶Clearly, barter is quite inefficient in comparison to money.

(Continues on next page)

____ 4. [1]Your sleep style is at least partly influenced by your personality and your gender. [2]According to Army research, people who are very sociable and physically active tend to be "short" sleepers (those who require six or fewer hours of sleep to feel refreshed). [3]Folks who are mainly introverted and mentally creative are more likely to be "long" sleepers (those who need more than eight hours). [4]It's thought that these people, because of the extra time they spend "in their head," are more aware of themselves and their inner conflicts than very social or physically oriented people might be. [5]And since dreams offer us an opportunity to work out problems, they need and use the extra dream time to resolve mental conflicts and puzzles. [6]The researchers further noted that women tend to awaken more frequently than men do and to sleep less soundly, as well. [7]It is speculated that the reason for this is biochemical, since women, through most stages of life, experience greater hormonal shifts than men do.

____ 5. [1]In Western society, adolescence is an often stormy period that frequently places parents and their children in conflict. [2]Adolescents are told to "act like adults," but they are often treated as children. [3]The Mbuti tribe of East Africa provides a practical solution to the problem of how to become an adult. [4]Mbuti boys and girls are taken from their homes to separate "marriage and adulthood" camps. [5]During the three months that the camps last, the children are taught about the responsibilities of adulthood. [6]They learn about sharing, conflict, and respecting others. [7]The elders of the community talk to them about spiritual and moral values. [8]When the "campers" return to their village, they are no longer boys and girls. [9]They are men and women entitled to marry and set up their own homes.

SUPPORTING DETAILS: Test A

A. Answer the questions or follow the directions for the textbook passages below.

[1]Stereotyping consists of assigning traits to people solely on the basis of a category. [2]Some researchers suggest that stereotyping has four clear phases. [3]First, a person distinguishes a particular category of people—for example, economists. [4]Second, the person notes that one or more of the people in this category have certain traits—for example, dullness. [5]Third, the person generalizes that everyone in this category has these characteristics—for example, that all economists are dull. [6]Finally, when meeting someone the person is not acquainted with but knows to be, for example, an economist, the person stereotypes this individual as dull.

____ 1. In general, the major supporting details of this paragraph are
   A. characteristics given to people solely on the basis of their class or category.
   B. people who have studied stereotypes.
   C. examples of stereotyping.
   D. the stages people go through when they stereotype.

____ 2. How many major details are in this paragraph?
   A. Two
   B. Three
   C. Four
   D. Five

____ 3. Sentence 2 provides
   A. the main idea.
   B. a major detail.
   C. a minor detail.

____ 4. Economists are used in the paragraph as
   A. the main idea.
   B. major details.
   C. minor details.

____ 5. According to some researchers, people who stereotype end up by judging
   A. phases.
   B. friends.
   C. acquaintances.
   D. individuals they are not acquainted with.

(Continues on next page)

¹There are three principal kinds of animal diets. ²In a carnivorous diet, animals feed on other animals. ³Most fish are carnivorous. ⁴So too are owls, snakes, and wolves. ⁵On a herbivorous diet, animals subsist on plant food. ⁶Cattle, Japanese beetles, seed-eating birds, and plant lice are among the many herbivores. ⁷With the omnivorous diet, animals have a mixed diet. ⁸They feed on both vegetable and animal matter, dead or alive. ⁹Many kinds of worms, crabs, lobsters, insects, bears and raccoons are omnivorous. ¹⁰Humans are also omnivores.

6. Complete the outline of the paragraph by filling in the missing major detail.

   There are three principal kinds of animal diets.

   1. Carnivorous (eat animals)
   2. _____
   3. Omnivorous (eat both animals and plants)

B. (7–10.) Complete the outline of the following paragraph by filling in the rest of the main idea and the major supporting details, including an explanation of each. One explanation has been done for you.

   ¹Burn injuries are classified in three categories, according to their severity. ²First-degree burns are burns that leave a painful red mark but do not break the skin, and thus they do not often become infected. ³Burns that are classified as second-degree burn through the skin, which develops blisters. ⁴Second-degree burns are often extremely painful, and, since the skin has been broken, they may become infected. ⁵In a third-degree burn, both the outer and lower layers of skin are burned. ⁶There may be little pain because nerve endings have been destroyed. ⁷Because so much of the skin's protection has been lost, the possibility of serious, even fatal infection is great with a third-degree burn.

   Main idea: There are three _____

   _____

   1. _____

   _____

   2. _____—burn through skin, causing blisters and often great pain and infection

   3. _____

   _____

SUPPORTING DETAILS: Test B

A. Answer the questions that follow the passage.

[1]Self-disclosure is a special type of conversation in which we share intimate information and feelings with another person. [2]There are many reasons why we disclose personal information to another person. [3]One is simply to express our feelings—to "get them off our chest." [4]After a hard day at work, we may eagerly tell a friend just how angry we are at our boss and how unappreciated we feel. [5]A second reason for self-disclosure is to gain greater understanding and self-awareness. [6]Talking to a friend about a problem can help us to clarify our thoughts about the situation. [7]Social approval is another reason for disclosing information. [8]By seeing how a listener reacts to what we say, we get information about the appropriateness of our views. [9]People may reassure us that our reactions are "perfectly normal" or suggest that we're "blowing things out of proportion." [10]Yet another common reason for self-disclosure is relationship development. [11]The sharing of personal information is an important way to begin a relationship and to move toward increasing levels of intimacy.

____ 1. The main idea is expressed in
  A. sentence 1.
  B. sentence 2.
  C. sentence 3.
  D. sentence 11.

____ 2. In general, the major details of the passage are
  A. ways to express our feelings.
  B. thoughts about the appropriateness of our views.
  C. ways to begin relationships.
  D. reasons we disclose information to others.

____ 3. How many major details are in this paragraph?
  A. Two
  B. Three
  C. Four
  D. Five

____ 4. The first major detail is introduced with the addition word
  A. *another.*
  B. *many.*
  C. *one.*
  D. *other.*

____ 5. Self-disclosure is a conversation in which
  A. we discuss anything of interest.
  B. our reactions are blown out of proportion.
  C. we share something personal.
  D. we discuss social approval.

(Continues on next page)

B. (6–10.) Complete the outline of the following paragraph by filling in the rest of the main idea and the missing major and minor supporting details.

[1]Although the debate continues over the influence of heredity, as opposed to environment, in human development, scientists have learned that a number of human characteristics clearly have genetic factors. [2]Physical traits are most strongly determined by heredity. [3]Height, obesity, and patterns of tooth decay are just a few of the traits that have been found to be determined by our genes. [4]Intellectual traits are also strongly influenced by genes. [5]For instance, research indicates that scores on intelligence tests and memory have a strong hereditary basis. [6]In addition, personality factors are greatly influenced by heredity. [7]Shyness and special talents and interests are all influenced by genetic transmission. [8]Even emotional disorders such as schizophrenia are affected by genes.

Main idea: A number of human characteristics have _____

    1. Physical traits

       Examples—height, obesity, and patterns of tooth decay

    2. _____

       Examples— _____

    3. _____

       Examples— _____

    4. Emotional disorders

       Example—schizophrenia

SUPPORTING DETAILS: Test C

A. (1–4.) Complete the map of the following textbook passage by filling in the main idea and the three missing major details, including an explanation of each. One explanation has been started for you.

[1]Psychologists use several theories to explain different sides of human behavior. [2]Best-known is the psychoanalytic theory, which holds that people are driven largely by needs and desires that they are not aware of—the so-called "subconscious" mind. [3]Another theory, behaviorism, suggests that people's actions are based largely on past experiences of reward and punishment. [4]We do things that brought us pleasant results in the past and avoid things that brought unpleasant results. [5]Yet another theory, "gestalt" psychology, emphasizes the role of overall patterns in our thinking. [6]For example, we find it much easier to remember a tune than a series of unconnected musical notes.

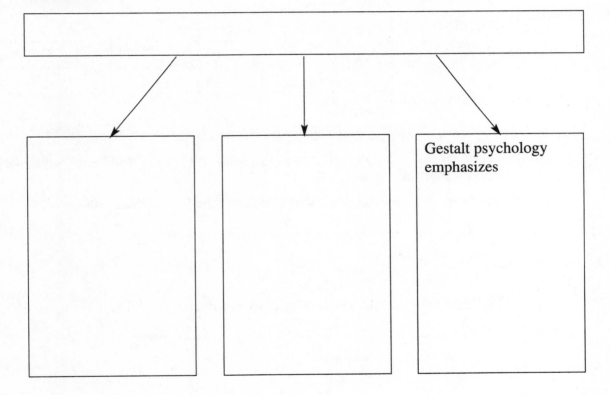

Gestalt psychology
emphasizes

(Continues on next page)

B. Carefully read the paragraph, and then answer the questions that follow.

> [1]People once thought that the mountains, plains, plateaus, and other features of the Earth had always existed. [2]But the science of geology reveals that two processes work continuously to shape and to alter the face of the Earth: the forces of construction and the forces of destruction. [3]The constructive forces are those that lift up the land masses to produce forms like mountains. [4]Earthquakes and volcanoes demonstrate the workings of constructive forces. [5]The destructive forces are those which cause the leveling down of mountains and hills. [6]The cutting action of running streams and the rubbing of glacial ice are some of the forces that reduce the high places of the Earth.

5. The main idea of the passage is expressed in sentence number _____.

___ 6. In general, the major details of this paragraph are
   A. geological features of the Earth.
   B. processes that shape and alter the face of the Earth.
   C. features of the Earth.
   D. the high places on Earth.

___ 7. Specifically, the major details of this paragraph are
   A. mountains, plains, plateaus, and other features of the Earth.
   B. shaping and altering.
   C. the Earth's constructive forces and destructive forces.
   D. earthquakes and volcanoes.

8. Mountains are produced by the Earth's _____ forces.

9–10. Complete the following outline of the paragraph by filling in the missing major and minor supporting details.

There are two processes that shape and alter the face of the Earth.

   A. _____

      1. Earthquakes

      2. Volcanoes

   B. Destructive forces, which level down mountains and hills

      1. _____

      2. Rubbing of glacial ice

Name _____

Section _____ Date _____

SCORE: (Number correct) × 10 = _____%

SUPPORTING DETAILS: Test D

A. (1–6.) Complete the map of the following paragraph by filling in the main idea and the five major supporting details.

[1]A number of factors contribute to the fact that poor people are less healthy than well-off people. [2]For one thing, low-income families tend to have less nutritious diets than higher-income families. [3]In particular, low-income diets are often deficient in the amount of protein which they provide. [4]Many poorer families probably have some level of malnutrition much of the time, a fact that influences their susceptibility to illness. [5]Second, the general standard of living among low-income groups is likely to be lower. [6]Their homes are more crowded, more likely to be in disrepair, and more often located in dangerous neighborhoods. [7]Another factor affecting health in poor people is that low-income families usually receive less medical care and lower-quality medical care than wealthier ones do. [8]Failure to have minor ailments cared for may make these people more likely to have major ailments later on. [9]Fourth, people with low incomes are probably under a lot of physical stress, a factor which appears to be related to the onset of illness. [10]Last of all, poor people are subject to a great deal of psychological stress, a factor that may be even more powerful than physical stress in leaving the body exposed to illness.

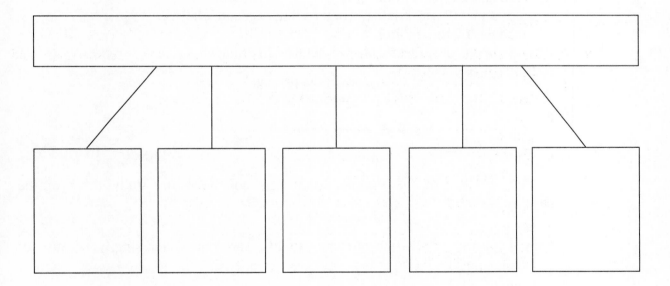

(Continues on next page)

B. After reading the textbook passage below, answer the questions or follow the directions.

> [1]The *mere exposure effect*—the tendency to like someone better simply because of frequent exposure to him or her—has been observed in studies. [2]In one study, college students were shown pictures of faces. [3]Some of the faces were shown as many as twenty-five times; others, only once or twice. [4]Afterward, subjects indicated how much they liked each face and how much they thought they would like the person pictured. [5]The more often the subjects had seen a face, the more they said they liked it and thought they would like the person. [6]The same result has been found for repeated exposure to actual people. [7]In a recent study, researchers enlisted the aid of four college women who served as confederates in an experiment. [8]A pretest showed that all women were rated as equally attractive. [9]In the study, each woman attended a large lecture class in social psychology, posing as a student in the course. [10]Each woman attended a different number of class sessions—once, five times, ten times, or fifteen times during the term. [11]At the end of the term, students in the class were asked to rate each woman, based on a casual photo shown as a slide. [12]The more often students had seen the woman, the more they thought they would like her.

7. *Fill in the blank:* The main idea of the paragraph is expressed in sentence _____.

____ 8. The supporting details are
    A. reasons to like someone.
    B. studies that illustrate and prove the mere exposure effect.
    C. examples of classroom behavior.
    D. ways in which students rate people they don't know.

____ 9. How many supporting details are in the passage?
    A. One
    B. Two
    C. Three
    D. Four

____10. Write the letter of the summary that best completes the study notes of the paragraph.

Study notes:

Mere exposure effect—the tendency to like someone better simply because of frequent exposure to him or her

Example—
    A. In one study, college students were shown pictures of faces, some as many as twenty-five times.
    B. The more often students saw each of four women in their class, the more they thought they would like her.
    C. Four women who were rated as equally attractive attended a large lecture class once, five, ten, or fifteen times during the term.

IMPLIED MAIN IDEAS: Test A

A. In the space provided, write the letter of the sentence that best expresses the implied main idea of each of the following paragraphs.

____ 1. [1]A puddle of dark liquid under a car indicates a leak in the oil or transmission fluid. [2]Another warning sign of car trouble is uneven wear on tire treads. [3]If the outer edge of the tire tread wears out before the center, the tire is under-inflated. [4]The most significant early warning signal, however, is less and less mileage per gallon. [5]Lower fuel economy is caused by a variety of problems ranging from a clogged filter to ignition or carburetor trouble.

   A. Several warning signs can indicate car problems.
   B. A puddle of dark liquid under a car is a sign that a car has an oil or transmission-fluid leak.
   C. The most significant warning signal of a car problem is getting lower mileage per gallon of gas.
   D. Various problems may cause a car's fuel economy to decrease.

____ 2. [1]We think of crime as having a clear victim who suffers at the hands of another person. [2]Some crimes, however, don't seem to have victims. [3]These victimless crimes include prostitution, illicit drug use, and gambling. [4]In this type of crime, there is usually no one who feels he or she has been harmed. [5]These acts are called criminal because the community as a whole, or powerful groups within it, regard them as morally wrong. [6]Those who hold different views of morality think that at least some of these behaviors should not be considered criminal. [7]Still others argue that victimless crimes really do have victims. [8]For example, compulsive gamblers rob their families of income. [9]Also, prostitutes spread AIDS and other sexually transmitted diseases, and drug users may resort to other crimes to support their habit.

   A. Victimless activities such as prostitution and gambling should not be illegal.
   B. The community or a powerful part of it determines what activities are criminal.
   C. There are varying views of victimless crimes.
   D. One view of victimless crimes is that they in fact do have victims.

____ 3. [1]A round foundation in Africa that is two million years old reveals an appreciation like our own for balance and form. [2]A flower arrangement found in an ancient burial site in Iraq suggests that flowers were a symbol of comfort. [3]Ice Age sculptures emphasize human sexuality, showing the importance of fertility to early people. [4]And cave paintings dating back to 20,000 B.C. prove that the artists were keen observers of nature.

   A. Ancient artists were even more talented than artists of recent centuries.
   B. Early human handiwork suggests that ancient peoples had values and sensitivities much like our own.
   C. An ancient flower arrangement at a burial site shows that flowers have been a symbol of comfort for centuries.
   D. Humans were interested in producing art as far back as 20,000 B.C.

(Continues on next page)

B. (4.) In the space provided, write the letter of the item that best expresses the implied central idea of the following passage.

_____ [1]At the beginning of the twentieth century, the United States was reaching adulthood. [2]Unequal distribution of wealth and income persisted. [3]One percent of American families possessed nearly seven-eighths of its wealth. [4]Four-fifths of Americans lived on a survival level while a handful lived in incredible luxury. [5]In 1900, Andrew Carnegie earned about $23 million; the average working man earned $500. [6]The wealth of a few was increased by the exploitation of women and children. [7]One out of five women worked for food rather than fulfillment, earning wages as low as $6 a week. [8]The sacrifice of the country's young to the god of economic growth was alarming. [9]One reporter undertook to do a child's job in the mines for one day and wrote, "I tried to pick out the pieces of slate from the hurrying stream of coal, often missing them; my hands were bruised and cut within a few minutes; I was covered from head to foot with coal dust, and for many hours afterwards I was expectorating some of the small particles of anthracite I had swallowed."

[10]Working conditions were equally horrifying in other industries, and for many Americans, housing conditions were as bad or worse. [11]One investigator described a Chicago neighborhood, remarking on the "filthy and rotten tenements, the dingy courts and tumbledown sheds, the foul stables and dilapidated outhouses, the broken sewer pipes, and piles of garbage fairly alive with diseased odors." [12]At the same time, the Vanderbilts summered in a "cottage" of seventy rooms, and wealthy men partied in shirts with diamond buttons worth thousands of dollars.

[13]The middle class experienced neither extreme. [14]Its members did have their economic grievances, however. [15]Prosperity increased the cost of living by 35 percent in less than a decade, while many middle-class incomes remained fairly stable. [16]Such people were not poor, but they believed they were not getting a fair share of the prosperity.

A. In 1901, the United States was finally becoming a strong country.
B. In 1901, the United States had three distinct classes of citizens: the rich, the middle class, and the poor.
C. At the beginning of the twentieth century, there were wide gaps between the income levels of America's rich and poor.
D. At the beginning of the twentieth century, a number of significant problems existed in the United States.

IMPLIED MAIN IDEAS: Test B

A. Write the letter of the sentence that best expresses the implied main idea of each of the following paragraphs.

_____ 1. [1]In the late 1980s, concern about the deadly effects of illegal drugs became a top national issue. [2]Politicians loudly proclaimed a "war on drugs," and TV news shows carried regular reports about the fatal toll of drugs, especially "crack" cocaine. [3]These drugs do have a terrible effect on individuals and society, but the facts about them are somewhat different from their popular image. [4]Each year, about two thousand people die from heroin overdoses, and about three thousand die from cocaine-related causes. [5]At the same time, 50,000 people die every year because of alcohol—including thousands of innocent victims of drunk drivers. [6]Additionally, a third of a million people die every year from cancer due to smoking cigarettes.

    A. In the late 1980s, politicians proclaimed a "war on drugs."

    B. Our "war on drugs" ignores the two deadliest (though legal) drugs, alcohol and tobacco.

    C. Thousands of people die each year from heroin overdoses and cocaine-related causes.

    D. More people die each year from alcohol-related causes than from cocaine-related causes.

_____ 2. [1]One reason tabloids publish untrue stories about celebrities, even though they know the celebrities might sue, is free advertising. [2]If there is a lawsuit, it will make the news, and the tabloid gains the publicity. [3]Furthermore, in a lawsuit the burden of proof is on the celebrity, not the paper. [4]Also, such lawsuits are both expensive and time-consuming. [5]A court delay, for example, can prevent a movie star from beginning work on a new project. [6]And the chances of collecting a significant amount of damages are slim. [7]Finally, tabloids publish untrue stories for the obvious reason: whether it is true or not, people love celebrity gossip—and it sells papers.

    A. Tabloids publish untrue stories about celebrities.

    B. Tabloids publish untrue stories about celebrities because celebrities will think twice about suing.

    C. There are a few reasons why tabloids publish untrue stories about celebrities, even though the celebrities might sue.

    D. Even if celebrities sue tabloids over untrue stories, they are unlikely to collect a lot of money for damages.

_____ 3. [1]In the past it often took years to force a car company to make even small, inexpensive changes. [2]In the 1960s, consumer advocate Ralph Nader had to fight for several years before Chevrolet stopped making the unsafe Corvair. [3]But in recent years, customer complaints and publicity have led to quick corrective actions. [4]For example, the Consumers Union recently reported that all-terrain

(Continues on next page)

vehicles (ATVs) were unsafe when driven by untrained operators. ⁵Within eighteen months, ATV makers stopped making unstable three-wheeled models and set up an extensive customer training program. ⁶More recently, *Consumer Reports* magazine revealed safety problems in the Ford Bronco II. ⁷In response, Ford immediately announced a complete redesign and the decision to market the re-engineered vehicle under a new name.

A. Companies should respond more quickly to changes demanded by consumer advocates.
B. Ralph Nader had to fight for years in the 1960s before Chevrolet stopped making the unsafe Corvair.
C. Because of customer complains and publicity, car manufacturers are correcting car problems more quickly than they once did.
D. If you want a product to be improved, take the responsibility of complaining to the company.

B. (4.) In the space provided, write the letter of the item that best expresses the implied central idea of the following textbook passage.

_____ ¹Our culture places a high premium on personal choice in matters of the heart. ²But in the rest of the world, personal choice is not the only path to marriage. ³In parts of India, for example, marriages are arranged by parents. ⁴Love is not viewed as an important basis for marriage there. ⁵When parents select a bride, they emphasize her good character, obedience, domestic skills, religiousness, and appearance. ⁶In selecting a groom, the social and economic standing of the family and the young man's education and earning potential are paramount.

⁷Teenagers in traditional societies often welcome their parents' help in selecting a mate. ⁸When girls in India learned about American marriage customs, they expressed serious concerns about the hazards of free choice. ⁹One girl asked if an American girl who is shy and does not call attention to herself might not get married. ¹⁰Another girl said it would be humiliating to have to attract a boy. ¹¹"It makes getting married a sort of competition in which the girls are fighting each other for the boys. ¹²And it encourages a girl to pretend she's better than she really is." ¹³Other girls praised their parents' judgment about a potential husband. ¹⁴"It's so important that the man I marry should be the right one. ¹⁵I could so easily make a mistake if I had to find him for myself."

¹⁶An anthropologist has painted a similar portrait of marriage in traditional Chinese culture. ¹⁷For centuries, it was common for Chinese marriages to be arranged by parents and hired go-betweens; the partners might not even meet until their wedding. ¹⁸Proponents of arranged marriage emphasize that parents are better judges of character than children and that passion is an unrealistic basis for marriage. ¹⁹They observe that well-matched partners from compatible families gradually learn to find love and satisfaction with each other.

A. Arranged marriages have fewer risks than marriages based on love and romance.
B. Arranged marriages are customary in many traditional societies, in which romance is not as important as character and economic and social standing.
C. Parents are much better at choosing mates for their children than the children are.
D. If arranged marriages became the norm in the United States, there would be fewer divorces.

IMPLIED MAIN IDEAS: Test C

A. Write the letter of the sentence that best expresses the implied main idea of each of the following passages.

____ 1. [1]During the 1989 Northern California earthquake, a half-mile section of elevated freeway in Oakland collapsed on itself. [2]Since the earthquake happened right at the afternoon rush hour, early estimates were that more than two hundred people might have died, crushed in the rubble. [3]But by sheer good luck, the earthquake came just before the scheduled start of a World Series baseball game between the Oakland "A's" and the San Francisco Giants. [4]Thousands of people had left work early to get home for the game. [5]Others went to friends' homes or bars near where they worked to watch the game, instead of driving straight home. [6]Thus, few people were on the freeway when the quake hit, and the death toll was much lower than expected.

    A. The 1989 Northern California earthquake came just before the scheduled start of a World Series game.

    B. Because of a scheduled World Series game, the death toll from the 1989 Northern California earthquake was lower than expected.

    C. Being on the freeway during an earthquake is more dangerous than being at home.

    D. Before the 1989 Northern California earthquake, many people left work early to watch the World Series.

____ 2. [1]How much water is stored as glacial ice? [2]Estimates by the U.S. geological survey indicate that only slightly more than 2 percent of the world's water is accounted for by glaciers. [3]But this small figure may be misleading when the actual amounts of water are considered. [4]The total volume of all valley glaciers is about 210,000 cubic kilometers. [5]That volume is comparable to the combined volume of the world's largest saltwater and freshwater lakes. [6]Furthermore, 80 percent of the world's ice and nearly two-thirds of the Earth's fresh water are represented by Antarctica's ice sheet, which covers an area almost one and one-half times that of the United States. [7]If this ice melted, sea level would rise an estimated sixty to seventy meters, and the ocean would flood many densely populated coastal areas. [8]The amount of the continent's ice can be illustrated in another way. [9]If Antarctica's ice sheet were melted at a uniform rate, it would feed (1) the Mississippi River for more than 50,000 years, (2) all the rivers in the United States for about 17,000 years, (3) the Amazon River for approximately 5,000 years, or (4) all the rivers of the world for about 750 years.

    A. If melted at a uniform rate, Antarctica's ice sheet would feed the Mississippi River for 50,000 years.

    B. The world's water takes various forms—salt water, fresh water, and ice.

    C. If Antarctica's glacial ice were melted, the ocean would flood many heavily populated coastal areas.

    D. The quantity of glacial ice on Earth today is truly immense.

(Continues on next page)

B. (3.) Write out the implied main idea of the following paragraph.

[1]Some researchers have found that women are more likely than men to use eye contact and smiles to attract members of the opposite sex. [2]Women also have a tendency to use fleeting touches and seductive grooming, such as lip licking and hair smoothing, as flirting signals. [3]In comparison, men rarely make these gestures for the same purpose. [4]Indeed, according to the researchers, the only flirting technique that men use frequently is the obvious, direct approach—hugging or kissing, which is as direct as you can get!

Implied main idea: _____

_____

C. (4.) In the space provided, write the letter of the item that best expresses the implied central idea of the following textbook passage.

_____ [1]In their research on happiness, psychologists have studied influences upon both our temporary moods and our long-term life satisfaction. [2]Studying people's reports of daily moods confirms that stressful events—an argument, a sick child, a car problem—trigger bad moods. [3]No surprise there. [4]But by the next day, the gloom nearly always lifts. [5]When in a bad mood, you can usually depend on rebounding within a day or two. [6]Similarly, your times of joy are hard to keep going.

[7]Apart from prolonged grief over the loss of a loved one or continuing anxiety after a traumatic stress, such as child abuse, rape, or the terrors of war, even tragedy is not permanently depressing. [8]The finding is surprising but reliable. [9]People who become blind or paralyzed usually recover near-normal levels of day-to-day happiness. [10]For example, able-bodied University of Illinois students described themselves as happy 50 percent of the time, unhappy 22 percent of the time, and neutral 29 percent of the time. [11]To within one percentage point, students with disabilities rated their emotions identically. [12]Moreover, students perceive their friends with disabilities as just as happy as their other friends.

[13]The effect of dramatically positive events is similarly temporary. [14]Once the rush of euphoria wears off, state lottery winners typically find their overall happiness is unchanged. [15]Other research confirms that there is much more to well-being than being well-off. [16]Many people believe they would be happier if they had more money. [17]They probably would be—temporarily. [18]But in the long run, increased wealth hardly affects happiness. [19]People with lots of money are not much happier than those with just enough money to afford life's necessities.

A. Psychologists have conducted many studies on the causes of happiness.
B. Psychologists have learned that money and happiness are not related.
C. Psychologists have learned that in the long run, our emotional ups and downs tend to wear off, and we go back to feeling as we always did.
D. According to psychologists, emotional ups and downs are a normal part of life.

IMPLIED MAIN IDEAS: Test D

A. Write the letter of the sentence that best expresses the implied main idea of each of the following textbook paragraphs.

___ 1. ¹Many companies sell tapes with subliminal messages, messages that are too faint to consciously hear. ²The companies promise that the tapes will "reprogram your unconscious mind for success and happiness." ³Is there anything to these wild claims? ⁴Some researchers decided to find out. ⁵They randomly assigned eager university students to listen daily for five weeks to commercial subliminal tapes designed to improve either self-esteem or memory. ⁶On half the tapes, the researchers switched the labels. ⁷People given these tapes thought they were receiving statements supporting self-esteem, when they actually heard the memory enhancement tape. ⁸Or they got the memory tape but thought their self-esteem was being recharged. ⁹Were the tapes effective? ¹⁰Scores on both self-esteem and memory tests, taken before and after the five weeks, revealed no effects at all.

A. According to one study, subliminal tapes that are sold with promises of self-improvement have no effects at all.

B. University students were assigned to listen to commercial subliminal tapes daily for five weeks.

C. Companies claim that subliminal tapes can positively influence one's success and happiness.

D. Many products do not live up to the claims made for them.

___ 2. ¹The University of California at Santa Cruz wanted undergraduates to conserve water by taking shorter showers. ²So they posted signs in the men's shower rooms urging bathers to "(1) wet down, (2) turn water off, (3) soap up, (4) rinse off." ³But only 6 percent of students complied with the posted request. ⁴A psychologist used conformity pressure to improve matters dramatically. ⁵He had an assistant wait in the shower room, poised to take a shower, until a student entered the room. ⁶Then the assistant showered, carefully following the instructions on the sign. ⁷Nearly half the students who encountered this energy-conscious assistant followed the recommended procedures. ⁸When there were two water-saving assistants, compliance by students increased to 67 percent.

A. A sign telling university students how to shower in order to conserve water was largely ignored.

B. All too often, signs asking for cooperation have little influence on citizens.

C. A good way of achieving the important goal of conserving water is to take shorter showers.

D. Conformity pressure did a much better job of getting students to conserve water than a sign alone did.

(Continues on next page)

B. (3.) Write out the implied main idea of the following paragraph.

    [1]Scientists have wondered for years how the monarch butterfly, an insect with a brain the size of a pinhead, can migrate almost two thousand miles from various points in North America to winter in California and Mexico. [2]To complicate the mystery, because of the monarch's short life span, the butterflies that migrate in the fall are a few generations removed from the ones that did it the year before. [3]Therefore, each monarch makes the journey home without the benefit of memory. [4]One more puzzling aspect of this insect has intrigued scientists throughout their studies: Out of all the butterflies in the world, the monarch is the only type that migrates.

Implied main idea: _____

_____

C. (4.) In the space provided, write the letter of the item that best expresses the implied central idea of the following textbook passage.

_____ [1]With horrific television and magazine images of air crashes in mind, many people prefer the safety of their own cars. [2]Of those who do fly, 44 percent report feeling fearful.
    [3]Ironically, the reality is that, mile for mile, U.S. travelers during the 1980s were twenty-six times more likely to die in a car crash than on a commercial flight. [4]In one study in the 1990s, major U.S. airlines carried more than one billion passengers on sixteen million flights without a single death. [5]For most air travelers, the most dangerous part of the journey is the drive to the airport.
    [6]Similarly, many people are likely to exaggerate the likelihood of shark attacks after watching the film *Jaws*, which is about a killer shark. [7]Or from seeing the faces of missing children on milk cartons, people may misjudge their child's risk of being abducted by a stranger. [8]The U.S. Justice Department reports that fewer than 1 in 100,000 children a year nationwide are abducted. [9](Almost all child snatchings are family-related.)
    [10]In 2001, the terrorist attacks in hijacked planes on the World Trade Center and the Pentagon caused many would-be international vacationers to stay home and brave dangerous highways instead. [11]The same fearful public continues to drive without seatbelts, smoke billions of cigarettes a year, guzzle alcohol, and devour foods that put people at risk for the greatest of killers—heart disease. [12]Also, while the public dreads a horrible nuclear accident (which after the 1986 Chernobyl disaster we can readily visualize), it accepts the less dramatic risk of coal-generated power, which quietly fuels acid rain and global warming.

A. People are much more fearful today than they were a generation ago.
B. More people die in automobile accidents every year than in plane crashes.
C. Cigarettes, alcohol, acid rain, and global warming do not pose as much danger to us as terrorist attacks and nuclear accidents.
D. Whether making travel plans or choosing foods, defining safety standards or evaluating environmental hazards, people often judge risks based on media images, not on statistical reality.

RELATIONSHIPS I: Test A

A. Fill in each blank with the appropriate transition word from the box. Use each transition once.

after	also	another
next	until	

1. [1]Abraham Lincoln grew a beard only _____ being elected to the presidency. [2]An eleven-year-old girl told him that with a beard he "would look a great deal better, for your face is so thin."

2. [1]Tina's father is an overly cautious parent. [2]He wants to know where she is every minute, and he won't let her drive his car _____ she is 20.

3. [1]In 1835 Halley's comet appeared and Mark Twain was born. [2]Twain predicted that he'd die when Halley's comet showed up again. [3]And he did die in 1910, the year of the comet's _____ appearance.

4. [1]Other boys like to collect normal things, like baseball cards, but my little brother Dwayne collects dead bugs. [2]He _____ collects loose chunks of sidewalk (which he insists on calling moon rocks).

5. [1]There have been many fictional captains. [2]One is Captain Marvel, the red-suited comic-strip superhero. [3]_____ is Captain Nemo, captain of the submarine in Jules Verne's *Twenty Thousand Leagues Under the Sea*.

(Continues on next page)

B. Fill in each blank with an appropriate transition word from the box. Use each transition once. Then answer the question that follows.

another	during	one
third		

¹Many people who do sit-ups may not be getting the full benefit of the exercise because they're doing them incorrectly. ²Here are three common sit-up errors—and what should be done instead. ³(6)_____ error is allowing the stomach muscles to bulge out, rather than tucking them in. ⁴Doing this repeatedly can cause the muscles to stay stuck out, rather than flattening, which is the goal. ⁵To make sure your stomach muscles are tucked in while exercising them, try pushing your tummy into your back—that's what it should feel like. ⁶(7)_____ error is not breathing while doing sit-ups. ⁷Many people instinctively hold their breath during physical exertion—so they don't get the oxygen necessary to fuel an effective workout. ⁸The proper (and easiest) way to breathe (8)_____ sit-ups is to inhale for the easy part (lowering your back) and then to exhale during the hard part (lifting yourself up). ⁹A (9)_____ error is keeping the legs straight, which uses—and can strain—the lower-back muscles, rather than making full use of the stomach muscles. ¹⁰For safer, more effective sit-ups, keep those knees bent.

____10. The main pattern of organization of the above paragraph is
   A. list of items.
   B. time order.

RELATIONSHIPS I: Test B

A. Write the letter of the answer that describes the relationship indicated by the italicized transition.

____ 1. *After* the magician's assistant shuts the closet door, the magician escapes from the closet through a door in the floor.

   The relationship of the first part of the sentence to the second part is one of
   A. addition.   B. time.

____ 2. It's impossible to do everything perfectly, and *moreover,* it's ridiculous to try.

   The relationship of the second part of the sentence to the first part is one of
   A. addition.   B. time.

____ 3. First the pinch-hitter selected a bat from the rack. *Then* he took a few practice swings.

   The relationship of the second sentence to the first is one of
   A. addition.   B. time.

____ 4. You can use various methods to get your listeners' attention. *For one thing,* you can tell a joke or an anecdote.

   The relationship of the second sentence to the first is one of
   A. addition.   B. time.

____ 5. Emotions have a physical basis in our hormone system. They are *also* grounded in our experience.

   The relationship of the second sentence to the first is one of
   A. addition.   B. time.

B. Read the passage and answer the question that follows.

   [1]The vocabulary of a society or a group tells us what kinds of things are important to it. [2]First of all, sociologists have often noted that although most of us think and speak only of "snow" and "ice," the Eskimos, or Inuit, have many different words for them—depending on whether snow is freshly fallen and fluffy or old and packed down, or hard or melting, and on whether ice is solid or cracking. [3]Skiers also have many terms for snow, and skaters speak (with awe) of "black ice." [4]Clearly, snow and ice are important to these groups. [5]As a final example, people in the nineteenth century had many terms for a horse-drawn vehicle: buggy, dogcart, hansom, barouche, landau, phaeton, and more. [6]These carriages were an important aspect of their world, though today the terms mean little to us—we have many terms, instead, for automobiles.

____ 6. The main pattern of organization of the paragraph is
   A. list of items.
   B. time order.

(Continues on next page)

C. Fill in each blank with an appropriate transition word from the box. Use each transition once. Then answer the question that follows.

as	finally	then

[1]A calorie is the amount of heat required to raise the temperature of a kilogram (about a quart) of water one degree Celsius. [2]To determine the number of calories in a portion of food, a technician uses a device called a bomb calorimeter. [3]This device has a chamber that rests in a container of water. [4]The food is placed in this chamber, which is (7)_____ filled with oxygen under high pressure. [5]Next, the food is set on fire. [6](8)_____ it burns, it gives off heat, and the temperature of the water in the container rises. [7](9)_____, the total rise in temperature is measured, giving the calorie content of the food.

10. The main pattern of organization of the paragraph is
    A. list of items.
    B. time order.

RELATIONSHIPS I: Test C

Read each textbook passage and answer the questions or follow the directions provided.

A. [1]Societies go through several stages in the production of goods. [2]In many less developed countries, most people produce their own products and then consume them. [3]As a society continues to grow, however, a person's or household's special talents are recognized. [4]For example, one person may be very good at carpentry, one at baking bread, and one at growing vegetables. [5]Soon an exchange process takes place: "I'll trade you my bread or several loaves of it for the table and chair you've just built. [6]Chances are, I can bake the bread better and faster than you can, and I know you can build the tables and chairs better than I." [7]Eventually, several households begin to produce surplus products beyond their immediate needs. [8]People produce more and more until they no longer have time to engage in exchange activity. [9]They then turn their products over to one person or to a store that agrees to handle all further exchange activities. [10]In this manner, a modern marketing system is created.

1. The main pattern of organization for the above selection is
   A. list of items.
   B. time order.

2. A transition that introduces one of the major details of the paragraph is

   _____.

B. [1]From observing chimpanzees in the wild, Jane Goodall made two important discoveries that brought her international fame. [2]One discovery was that chimps make and use tools. [3]As Goodall looked on, for instance, several chimps plucked long blades of grass, stripped off the leaves, licked one end to make it sticky, and poked the stem into a termite nest, pulling it out covered with termites. [4]These they licked off as a child would a lollipop.

   [5]In addition, Goodall discovered that chimpanzees eat meat—on a regular basis. [6]Goodall frequently saw them catch, kill, and devour bushbucks and bushpigs. [7]She also saw them frequently kill and eat monkeys and young baboons. [8]Moreover, Goodall saw her chimps throw rocks and use sticks as clubbing weapons.

___ 3. The main pattern of organization for the above selection is
   A. list of items.
   B. time order.

___ 4. The words that introduce the major supporting details of the passage are
   A. *as, for instance, moreover.*
   B. *one, in addition.*
   C. *frequently, also.*

(Continues on next page)

5–6. Complete the outline of the passage.

Main idea: Jane Goodall made two important discoveries about chimps.

Major supporting details:

1. _____

2. _____

C. (7–10.) Complete the map of the following textbook passage.

¹In some ways, the American criminal-justice system is like a "wedding cake" with four layers, each layer representing a different kind of case. ²In the top layer are notorious criminal cases that get heavy news coverage. ³Our image of the justice system—of elaborate trials, highly paid defense lawyers, endless appeals—is formed by these cases, but they are only a small fraction of the total. ⁴The second layer down is made up of other serious felonies—murders, rapes, robberies—that don't get as much news coverage. ⁵Most of these cases are "plea-bargained," but usually result in prison terms. ⁶In the next layer are "less serious" felonies, such as car theft, that may not result in prison terms. ⁷Finally, the lowest and largest layer is made up of the huge number of misdemeanors, such as traffic violations. ⁸These cases are handled in a routine way, and they seldom result in jail terms.

The American Criminal-Justice System

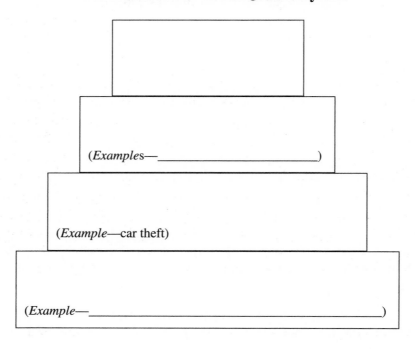

(*Examples*—_____)

(*Example*—car theft)

(*Example*—_____)

RELATIONSHIPS I: Test D

Read each textbook passage and answer the questions or follow the directions provided.

A. [1]In surveys of what people think about advertising, one of the most common and consistent complaints is that it is annoying to see the same old stuff over and over again. [2]Yet even though repetitive advertising is regarded as irritating, there are a couple of reasons why advertisers continue to use it. [3]First of all, repeated ads are cost-efficient. [4]With the high cost of creating and producing new advertising ideas and slogans, it makes sense to stick with proven winners. [5]In addition, the familiarity brought about by repeated exposure to advertising has been found to create attraction and liking. [6]How familiarity can result in sales can be seen in a typical trip to the grocery store in search of a laundry detergent. [7]We go to the detergent section and see a staggering array of brand names. [8]Because it doesn't much matter which one is purchased, we may simply reach for the most familiar one—and chances are it is familiar because we've heard and seen the name on television commercials over and over again. [9]Research studies have confirmed that more exposure results in increased liking.

____ 1. The main pattern of organization of the selection is
    A. list of items.
    B. time order.

2. The major supporting details of the paragraph are introduced with the transitions *first of all* and _____.

B. [1]According to most social psychologists, stereotypes are basically false for three reasons. [2]First of all, they exaggerate the differences between groups (for example, Irishmen are drunks; Jews don't drink), and they take no account of the millions of individual differences within groups. [3]Furthermore, they often carry the totally unproven assumption that the group's behavior is biologically determined. [4]Third, many of the traits assigned through stereotyping are simply not there. [5]For example, contrary to popular opinion, homosexuals do not have a distinct personality type. [6]According to research, most homosexuals are indistinguishable from heterosexuals in personality as well as in manner and appearance. [7]Also, women are not the bad drivers many believe they are. [8]Every year the percentage of women drivers responsible for automobile accidents is much smaller than the percentage of male drivers causing accidents.

____ 3. The main pattern of organization of the selection is
    A. list of items.
    B. time order.

4. The main idea is stated in sentence number _____.

5. The major supporting details are signaled with the transitions *first of all,* _____, and *third.*

(Continues on next page)

___ 6. The minor supporting details are
   A. steps.
   B. events.
   C. examples.

C. ¹Failure to cope adequately with organizational stress may lead to burnout. ²The burnout process occurs gradually. ³In fact, experts describe five stages of burnout. ⁴Stage one is the honeymoon. ⁵Beginning a new career is an exciting challenge. ⁶Learning to adapt to your new environment absorbs an enormous amount of valuable energy, but during this period you also must learn to adapt to stress. ⁷If you fail to do so, then you may move to the second stage. ⁸For many people, stage two begins with a vague realization that the honeymoon is over. ⁹Enthusiasm for the job begins to fade, and job dissatisfaction, inefficiency, fatigue, sleep disturbances, and escape activities may begin to bother you. ¹⁰Stage three of job burnout is marked by physical and psychological symptoms: chronic exhaustion, physical illness, anger and depression. ¹¹This may be when you first realize that you are in trouble. ¹²By stage four, symptoms become critical. ¹³Pessimism and frustration take over, and as a victim of burnout, you are obsessed with escaping. ¹⁴Finally, for the victim of professional burnout, stage five probably means that alcoholism, drug abuse, or heart disease have emerged as serious problems.

___ 7. The main pattern of organization for the above selection is
   A. list of items.
   B. time order.

8–10. Complete the map of the paragraph by adding the missing words to the main idea and filling in the missing major details.

   Main idea: According to experts, the burnout that results from organizational stress takes place in _____.

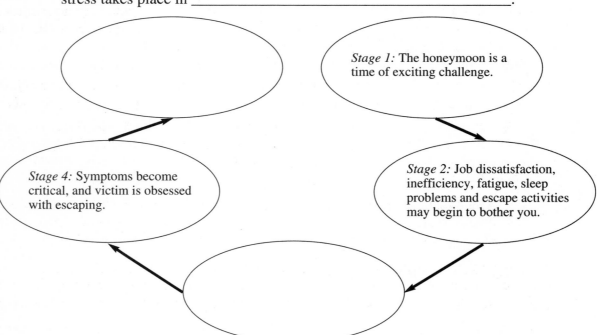

Stage 1: The honeymoon is a time of exciting challenge.

Stage 4: Symptoms become critical, and victim is obsessed with escaping.

Stage 2: Job dissatisfaction, inefficiency, fatigue, sleep problems and escape activities may begin to bother you.

RELATIONSHIPS II: Test A

A. Fill in each blank with an appropriate transition from the box. Use each transition once.

despite	for example	however
reason	similar	

1. [1]Plants can be surprisingly destructive. [2]Invading plants, _____, can relatively quickly turn an abandoned factory site into a field and then into woodland. [3]Dense vegetation completely overwhelms abandoned cities, especially in tropical areas, and the cities can be lost for centuries.

2. [1]Today, beach towns are popular tourist resorts. [2]_____, until a couple of hundred years ago, the seacoast was a place of danger. [3]People stayed away from the coast because they feared capture by pirates or slave-raiders. [4]In fact, many of the places we might like to go to in order to "get away" on vacation were once feared and avoided. [5]Have you ever daydreamed of being stranded on a tropical island? [6]That was once no daydream, but a terrible punishment for sailors found guilty of mutiny.

3. [1]Clothing is not only a means of keeping warm and decently covered; it's also a means of communication. [2]We affect others' perceptions of us by the way we dress. [3]If we are trying to establish ourselves as part of a group, we adopt the dress style of that group. [4]That's the _____ an applicant for an executive position shows up for the interview dressed like an executive: dark suit, conservative shoes, subdued jewelry.

4. [1]In the early days of industrialized America, many children worked full-time in factories and even mines. [2]_____ their small size and youth, children would often work up to fourteen hours a day. [3]Work conditions were often brutal, with children subjected to such horrors as being chained to their beds at night and to their factory machines during the day.

5. [1]Try the following experiment. [2]Ask a friend to drop a large handful of loose papers in the middle of a busy sidewalk, pretending that it is an accident. [3]Observe from afar how many people stop to help your friend pick up the papers. [4]Then try the same thing a second time, using the same or a _____ location at a similarly busy hour. [5]This time, however, you should help pick up the papers, all the while pretending to be a stranger. [6]You will probably find that when you help, others are more likely to help, too.

(Continues on next page)

B. Label each item with the letter of its main pattern of organization.

    A Definition and example
    B Comparison and/or contrast
    C Cause and effect

_____ 6. [1]Artificial intelligence (AI) is a term that describes computer programs that solve problems by "thinking" the way people do. [2]Most of these programs are based on sets of rules similar to logical thinking. [3]One AI program, for instance, was designed to diagnose infectious diseases. [4]It is about as efficient as most doctors. [5]In some fields, such as geology, AI programs have solved problems far more quickly than people could.

_____ 7. [1]The high cost of college today causes problems for many students in more ways than one. [2]For one thing, it undoubtedly prevents some students from attending college in the first place. [3]Also, high tuitions affect the amount of time available for studying; because loans and scholarships are hard to get, many students have to put in numerous hours at work in order to afford school. [4]Finally, those who do manage to get loans know that they must begin their careers with large debts.

_____ 8. [1]Back in 1800, American farmers worked 56 hours for every acre of wheat they raised. [2]In return, they harvested an average of 15 bushels for each hard-worked acre. [3]Today American farmers farm their wheat fields while riding in the air-conditioned cabs of huge diesel tractors and self-propelled combines. [4]It takes them an average of 2.8 hours a year to farm an acre of wheat. [5]And they average 31.4 bushels from each acre: twice as much wheat in 5 percent as many hours of work.

_____ 9. [1]An eidetic memory is the ability to recall every detail of a memory as clearly as if one were looking at a photograph. [2]An interesting example is the law student with eidetic memory who was accused of cheating on an examination because his test paper contained exactly the words in his textbook. [3]To prove his innocence, he studied an unfamiliar passage for five minutes and then wrote down more than four hundred words from it without making a mistake.

_____ 10. [1]When rangeland is overgrazed, the natural vegetation is destroyed and undesirable species take over. [2]If cattle herds graze on rangeland, they trample young plants, preventing their growth. [3]They also compact soil so that seeds cannot sprout. [4]This results in a reversion to an earlier stage of development, in which colonizing plants (usually undesirable) enter an area. [5]In addition, overgrazing accelerates erosion as topsoils are washed away, along with minerals and other nutrients.

RELATIONSHIPS II: Test B

Read each paragraph and answer the questions that follow.

A. [1]If you can't get rid of a cold, the flu, or a nagging sore throat, the reason may be your toothbrush. [2]Studies at the University of Oklahoma Dental School have shown that your old toothbrush may carry the germs that are causing your illness. [3]The studies have found that people who change their toothbrushes about every two weeks recover from common winter ills faster than people who use their toothbrushes for a month or more. [4]Old toothbrushes can culture the germs that can cause colds, influenza, pneumonia, strep throat, diarrhea, and sinus disease. [5]Another study found that disease germs can live in an unused toothbrush for as long as a week. [6]They can start to thrive again every time you brush your teeth.

___ 1. The main pattern of organization of the selection is
   A. definition and example.
   B. cause and effect.
   C. comparison and/or contrast.

2. One transition that signals the pattern of organization is _____.

B. [1]Identical twins Jack Yufe and Oskar Stohr shared the same genes. [2]They were separated at six months of age, when their parents divorced. [3]Yufe was raised as a Jew, joined an Israeli kibbutz in his youth, and served in the Israeli navy. [4]Stohr was brought up as a Catholic and later became involved in the Hitler youth movement. [5]Despite the differences in their backgrounds, when they first met at the airport, both sported mustaches and two-pocket shirts and epaulets, and each carried a pair of wire-rimmed glasses with him. [6]Both read magazines from back to front. [7]Both excel at sports and have difficulty with math. [8]And both have similar personality profiles as measured by the Minnesota Multiphasic Personality Inventory.

___ 3. The main pattern of organization of the selection is
   A. definition and example.
   B. cause and effect.
   C. comparison and/or contrast.

4. One transition that signals the pattern of organization is _____.

(Continues on next page)

C. ¹"Regulators" are the subtle signals we use to control the give and take of conversation. ²In meetings, for example, you may lean forward, raise your index finger in midair, draw in a breath, and look directly at the speaker to signal that you want to speak next. ³If the speaker is willing to relinquish the floor, she will look at you, drop her own midair gesture, and lean back in her chair. ⁴If she is unwilling to relinquish the floor, she will probably raise her voice, accelerate her speech, and perhaps touch your arm to "squelch" you if you're close enough or give you a "wait a minute" hand gesture. ⁵All of these signals are sent subtly and quickly, usually without premeditation.

____ 5. The main pattern of organization of the selection is
  A. definition and example.
  B. cause and effect.
  C. comparison and/or contrast.

6. The transition that signals the pattern of organization is _____.

D. ¹Female employment and small families make divorce more likely in modern societies. ²A major result of the massive entry of women into the labor force has been to decrease the dependence of wives on their husbands for economic support. ³This change has had beneficial effects. ⁴For instance, woman need no longer cling to a brutal or drunken husband merely because she has nowhere else to turn. ⁵But it also encourages some women to give up on a relationship more quickly. ⁶Also, husbands have greater economic freedom to divorce wives who work because working wives are seldom granted a great deal of alimony.

____ 7. The main pattern of organization of the selection is
  A. definition and example.
  B. cause and effect.
  C. comparison and/or contrast.

8. One transition that signals the pattern of organization is _____.

E. ¹In Third World cities, poverty and affluence exist side by side. ²Skyscrapers tower over slums, and shantytowns spring up next door to luxurious apartment blocks and villas, continental restaurants, and nightclubs. ³In most Third World cities, a small middle and upper class lives in an affluent style familiar to their American and European counterparts. ⁴They own color televisions and VCRs, send their children to private schools, wear Italian suits and French fashions, and drive Japanese or German cars. ⁵Indeed, they have privileges beyond the reach of most middle-class Americans, such as full-time, live-in household help (which they can afford because of the large numbers of unemployed). ⁶At the opposite extreme are the great majority of urban residents. ⁷They live in quite different conditions most Americans cannot imagine—not only without electricity, but without solid buildings, streets, sewers, toilets, or even running water.

____ 9. The main pattern of organization of the selection is
  A. definition and example.
  B. cause and effect.
  C. comparison and/or contrast.

10. One transition that signals the pattern of organization is _____.

Name _____

Section _____ Date _____

SCORE: (Number correct) × 10 = _____%

RELATIONSHIPS II: Test C

Read each paragraph and answer the questions that follow.

A. [1]A psychology professor introduced the same male guest lecturer to two different classes. [2]The first class was told to expect a rather cold, dull, uninteresting person. [3]The second class was told to expect a warm, intelligent, friendly lecturer. [4]The lecturer presented identical information in the same manner to both groups. [5]The first group found his lecture boring and did not ask questions; the second group found him warm and stimulating and asked many questions. [6]This experiment has been replicated successfully many times. [7]The outcome of these experiments suggests that telling someone what to perceive in another person will influence what is experienced.

____ 1. The main idea of the paragraph is expressed in
   A. sentence 1.
   B. sentence 4.
   C. sentence 7.

____ 2. The two patterns of organization of the selection are comparison-contrast and
   A. definition and example.
   B. cause and effect.

B. [1]In selective perception, we tend to see, hear and believe only what we want to see, hear, and believe. [2]As the late Canadian philosopher Marshall McLuhan pointed out, "Everyone has his own set of goggles," and we all think that what we see with our set of goggles is what everyone else sees. [3]Many studies have demonstrated selective perception at work. [4]One involved showing people an editorial cartoon from a Northern newspaper ridiculing the Ku Klux Klan; the cartoon was repeatedly interpreted as pro-Klan when shown to Southern Klan sympathizers. [5]A classic example of selective perception appeared in the early 1970s when television producer Norman Lear introduced the bigot Archie Bunker to American television audiences in the situation comedy *All in the Family.* [6]Bunker's prejudices were reflected in a number of controversial topics, such as sex, religion, and racism. [7]The character of Archie Bunker was designed to satirize American bigotry. [8]But what developed were Archie Bunker fan clubs and Archie Bunker T-shirts proclaiming America's number-one television bigot a folk hero. [9]Many people thought what he said was true and thus failed to get the message or see the satire.

____ 3. Which statement best expresses the main idea of the selection?
   A. Selective perception is the tendency to see, hear and believe only what we want to see, hear, and believe.
   B. The character of Archie Bunker was designed to satirize American bigotry.
   C. Bigots tend to interpret satire of prejudice as praise for bigotry.

____ 4. The paragraph mainly
   A. defines and illustrates "selective perception."
   B. explains the effects of bigotry.
   C. compares bigots with nonbigots.   *(Continues on next page)*

_____ 5. The supporting details of the paragraph are
   A. reasons.
   B. contrasts.
   C. examples.

C. [1]Sociologists have identified several common reasons why people join cults. [2]Many cult members come from homes filled with conflict; seeking to escape that conflict, they are drawn to the apparent security and acceptance offered by the cult. [3]Another reason people join a cult is that they may be overwhelmed by the demands of adult life. [4]The cult, with its strict rules and rigid discipline, relieves them from many personal decisions. [5]Finally, many cult members are highly idealistic persons—they are gratified by the feeling that by joining the cult, they are committing their lives to the establishment of a better world.

_____ 6. The two patterns of organization of the paragraph are list of items and
   A. definition and example.
   B. cause and effect.
   C. comparison and/or contrast.

7–10. Complete the map of the paragraph.

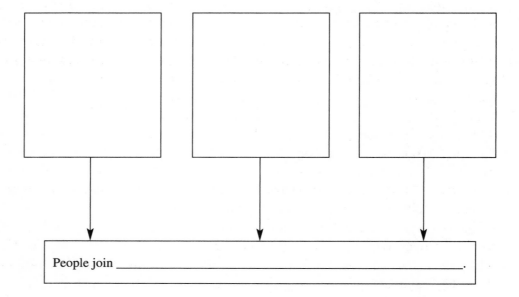

People join _____ .

RELATIONSHIPS II: Test D

Read each paragraph and answer the questions or follow the directions provided.

A. [1]Unfortunately, 60 percent of all new businesses will not celebrate a sixth anniversary. [2]Why do some small businesses fail? [3]Although there is no set pattern, there are four common causes of failure. [4]First is managerial incompetence or inexperience. [5]Many businesses are started by people with little or no management training or experience. [6]Some people think that management is just "common sense." [7]But if managers do not know how to make basic business decisions, they are unlikely to be successful in the long run. [8]The second common cause of failure is neglect. [9]After the glamour and excitement of the grand opening, some entrepreneurs get discouraged and fail to focus on business as much as they should. [10]In short, starting a small business requires an overwhelming time commitment. [11]Small business owners who are unwilling to work long hours and perform many different functions are likely to fail. [12]A third common cause of failure is weak control systems. [13]A control system helps owners and managers monitor costs, production rates, productivity, and so forth. [14]If control systems do not signal approaching problems, managers may be in serious trouble before more visible difficulties alert them. [15]Finally, insufficient capital may contribute to failure. [16]Here is an oft-cited rule of thumb: A new business should have enough capital to operate at least six months without earning a profit. [17]Owners of new businesses are almost certain to fail if they expect to pay the second month's rent from the first month's profits.

_____ 1. The patterns of organization of the paragraph are list of items and
   A. definition and example.
   B. cause and effect.
   C. comparison and/or contrast.

2–4. Complete the outline of the paragraph by adding the missing words to the main idea and filling in the two missing major details.

   Main idea: There are four _____

   _____

   1. Managerial incompetence or inexperience

   2. _____

   3. _____

   4. Insufficient capital

(Continues on next page)

B. [1]Cities in developing countries are noticeably different from those in wealthier nations. [2]Visitors often comment on the number of younger people in the less developed countries. [3]Almost half of all city residents in these countries are children and young people, as compared to less than one quarter of the population of cities in developed countries. [4]Also, many unskilled workers found jobs in European and North American cities when the economies there became industrialized. [5]In contrast, one quarter of the work force is unemployed in a typical city in a developing country. [6]Although homeless people are found in Europe and North America, many more people live on the street and in improvised shacks in the less-developed nations. [7]In Mexico City, for instance, more than four million squatters live in improvised shelters.

5. The main idea of the selection is stated in sentence number _____.

____ 6. The main pattern of organization of the selection is
   A. definition and example.
   B. cause and effect.
   C. comparison and/or contrast.

7–10. Complete the chart of the paragraph by filling in the missing heading and details.

	Cities in Wealthier Nations	_____ _____
Younger people	Less than one quarter of population	_____ _____
Employment	Jobs for many unskilled workers	_____ _____
_____	Some on the streets	Many more on the streets and in shacks

INFERENCES: Test A

A. After reading each selection below, write the letter of the best answer to each question.

[1]In colonial America, anyone could become a physician merely by adopting the label. [2]There were no medical schools or medical societies to license or regulate what was a free-for-all trade. [3]Sometimes clergymen tried to provide medical care to their parishioners, and care of a sort was offered by all kinds of laypeople as well. [4]Documents of the time record a doctor who sold "tea, sugar, olives, grapes, anchovies, raisins, and prunes" along with medicinals. [5]Documents also tell of a woman who "Acts here in the Double Capacity of a Doctoress and Coffee Woman." [6]Training for medical practice, such as it was, was given by apprenticeship.

____ 1. The passage suggests that in comparison to today, a medical practice in colonial America
   A. must have been harder to establish.
   B. probably required more study.
   C. was less likely to be full-time.

____ 2. Considering the medical training and care, we might conclude that in colonial America
   A. most doctors did medical research.
   B. people were lucky to get good medical care.
   C. very few people would have been considered qualified to be medical apprentices.

[1]CPR—or cardiopulmonary resuscitation—is a life-saving procedure that forces oxygen-rich blood through a body in which the heart has stopped. [2]A person is not "dead" until his or her brain has died, which happens after about six minutes once the heart has stopped pumping blood through the brain. [3]When a qualified person does CPR, he or she presses on the patient's chest, squeezing the stopped heart between the breast bone and the spine, which forces blood through the body. [4]Between each series of pumps, the rescuer breathes into the victim's mouth, sending fresh oxygen into his lungs and into the blood. [5]Many people are alive today because of CPR.

____ 3. After someone's heart has stopped,
   A. people on the scene should wait for medical personnel to do CPR.
   B. CPR must be performed within about six minutes.
   C. CPR must be performed at a hospital.

____ 4. Essentially, CPR duplicates some of the activity of the
   A. brain.
   B. spine.
   C. heart.

(Continues on next page)

_____ 5. Pumping blood through the body during CPR is not enough because
        A. the pumping involves pressing on the patient's chest.
        B. the blood needs to receive oxygen.
        C. the pumped blood eventually reaches the brain.

B. (6–10.) Below is the beginning of an essay titled "The Plot Against People" by *New York Times* columnist Russell Baker. After reading the passage, check the **five** statements which are most logically supported by the information given.

inanimate: lifeless   *idle:* not busy
classified: grouped   *cunning:* slyness

¹Inanimate objects are classified scientifically into three major categories—those that break down, those that get lost, and those that don't work.

²The goal of all inanimate objects is to resist man and ultimately to defeat him, and the three major classifications are based on the method each object uses to achieve its purpose. ³As a general rule, any object capable of breaking down at the moment when it is most needed will do so. ⁴The automobile is typical of this category.

⁵With the cunning peculiar to its breed, the automobile never breaks down while entering a filling station which has a large staff of idle mechanics. ⁶It waits until it reaches a downtown intersection in the middle of the rush hour, or until it is fully loaded with family and luggage on the Ohio Turnpike. ⁷Thus it creates maximum inconvenience, frustration, and irritability. . . .

⁸Many inanimate objects, of course, find it extremely difficult to break down. ⁹Pliers, for example, and gloves and keys are almost totally incapable of breaking down. ¹⁰Therefore, they have had to evolve a different technique for resisting man.

¹¹They get lost. ¹²Science has still not solved the mystery of how they do it, and no man has ever caught one of them in the act.

_____ 1. We can conclude that the author does not own an automobile anymore.

_____ 2. The author writes about "inanimate objects," but describes them as having some characteristics of living beings.

_____ 3. The author has probably had frustrating experiences with things that broke down, got lost, and didn't work.

_____ 4. The author assumes his readers have had frustrating experiences with things breaking down, getting lost, and not working.

_____ 5. The essay appears to be about all types of "inanimate objects," both manmade and objects found in nature.

_____ 6. The passage's humor partly stems from the author's exaggerations.

_____ 7. We can conclude from the essay that the author often writes about science.

_____ 8. The passage's humor partly stems from the truth behind the author's points.

_____ 9. When the author refers to science and scientific classification, he expects to be taken seriously.

_____ 10. In real life, the author tends to lose things more often than others do.

Name _____

Section _____ Date _____

SCORE: (Number correct) × 10 = _____%

INFERENCES: Test B

A. Following is a poem by the American writer Stephen Crane (1871–1900). Read it, and then write the letters of the inferences which are most logically supported by the poem.

I Stood Upon a High Place

I stood upon a high place,
And saw, below, many devils
Running, leaping,
And carousing in sin.
One looked up, grinning,
And said, "Comrade! Brother!"

____ 1. In saying he "stood upon a high place," the speaker suggests that he felt
    A. more righteous than the devils he saw.
    B. jealous of the playful devils.
    C. beneath the devils he saw.

____ 2. In saying "Comrade! Brother!" the devil means to imply that
    A. the speaker is an angel.
    B. the speaker is friendly.
    C. the speaker is also a sinner.

B. After reading the passage below, write the letter of the best answer to each question.

[1]One wintry night in 1890, about four hundred Indians set up camp near Wounded Knee Creek, South Dakota. [2]When they awoke the next morning, they found themselves surrounded by U.S. soldiers. [3]On the hilltop above were numerous machine guns. [4]When the soldiers ordered the Indians to hand over any weapons they might have, the Indians refused. [5]The soldiers began searching for weapons. [6]Then someone fired a shot. [7]Immediately, the machine guns started blasting—cutting down Indian men, women, and children. [8]Within a short time, all were killed. [9]Several days later, the frozen bodies were tossed into a common grave. [10]Instead of condemning the soldiers, the government awarded the troop twenty-six Medals of Honor and labeled the event a "battle." [11]It was the last fought against the American Indian.

____ 3. The passage suggests that
    A. the first shot was fired by a U.S. soldier.
    B. the first shot was fired by an Indian man.
    C. historians don't know who fired the first shot.

____ 4. We can conclude that the author feels
    A. the U.S. soldiers deserved the Medals of Honor.
    B. the event was more of a massacre than a battle.
    C. the Indians were given a fair chance to avoid being shot down.

(Continues on next page)

C. (5–10.) After reading the passage below, check the **six** statements which are most logically supported by the information given.

¹Our heartbeat, sleeping habits, brain activity, body temperature, and much more operate in certain rhythms or cycles. ²Scientists called chronobiologists try to understand how our "internal clocks" operate to regulate such cycles. ³One experiment conducted by chronobiologists involved placing a twenty-seven-year-old woman in an underground cave for 130 days. ⁴She was cut off from any way to measure the passage of time—there was no natural light in the cave, nor any clocks. ⁵The temperature was a constant sixty-nine degrees. ⁶When the woman was brought out of the cave at the end of the four-month period, her sleep cycle had changed dramatically. ⁷She would stay awake twenty to twenty-five hours, then sleep about ten hours. ⁸Her menstrual cycle had stopped. ⁹She believed she had been in the cave for only two months.

_____ 1. Chronobiologists are apparently biologists who specialize in human rhythms and cycles.

_____ 2. The experiment suggests that the human "internal clock" is influenced by such external cues as light and temperature changes.

_____ 3. The woman in the experiment never returned to the condition she was in before the experiment.

_____ 4. The woman spent four months in total darkness.

_____ 5. In the absence of a clock or the natural light and darkness of a day, it can be hard to judge how much time has passed.

_____ 6. Experiments can reveal much about human behavior that is not otherwise readily apparent.

_____ 7. Some of the effects on the woman in the experiment probably resulted from having no exercise at all for 130 days.

_____ 8. The researchers probably considered sixty-nine degrees to be a pretty comfortable temperature for humans.

_____ 9. The rhythm of the human body is usually not influenced by the natural rhythm of a day on Earth.

_____ 10. The woman in the experiment probably planned for numerous activities to keep her busy and interested while she was in the cave.

INFERENCES: Test C

A. After reading the textbook selection, write the letter of the best answer to each question.

¹A century ago, a federal statute known as the Comstock Law made it illegal to distribute birth-control information and materials through the mails. ²Druggists who sold contraceptive devices were arrested. ³Various states had their own legislation concerning contraception. ⁴Some made it a crime to distribute contraceptive literature. ⁵Others forbade physicians to prescribe contraceptive devices. ⁶Some even (as in Connecticut) made it against the law for couples—single or married—to use contraceptive devices.

⁷Many of these anticontraceptive measures continued into the present century, some until recently. ⁸The clergy denounced birth control as sinful. ⁹Theodore Roosevelt warned of "race suicide." ¹⁰Condoms were referred to as "rubber articles for immoral use." ¹¹In the 1920s, the birth-control-movement leader Margaret Sanger needed diaphragms to distribute to women who came to her birth-control clinic. ¹²She was unable to obtain such contraceptives in the United States and had to purchase them from abroad. ¹³American manufacturers were by then permitted to manufacture contraceptive devices. ¹⁴But they refused to make the reliable Mensinga diaphragm and, instead, made unsatisfactory cervical caps. ¹⁵However, it was illegal to import contraceptives. ¹⁶Margaret Sanger's clinic therefore obtained them through illegal channels. ¹⁷The diaphragms were imported from Germany by way of Canada and then smuggled across the border in oil drums.

_____ 1. Roosevelt's warning of "race suicide" suggests that some opponents of contraception believed
    A. unmarried people should have children.
    B. there was no reliable way to prevent conception.
    C. if contraception were allowed, a low birthrate might lead to extinction.

_____ 2. The passage clearly implies that in the 1920s,
    A. women were content to let men handle contraception.
    B. some women were willing to risk arrest in order to get good contraceptives.
    C. most women were not religious at all.

_____ 3. From the passage we can conclude that in the 1920s,
    A. men led the birth-control movement.
    B. American contraceptive manufacturers did not fully respond to the demands of the market.
    C. the Comstock Law was still valid.

_____ 4. We can conclude that
    A. in reality, American laws about birth control have changed very little since a century ago.
    B. throughout the twentieth century, religious leaders had the most influence on views about birth control.
    C. many Americans' views on birth control have changed since the Comstock Law.

(Continues on next page)

B. (5–10.) After reading the textbook passage below, check the **six** statements which are most logically supported by the information given.

¹Maria Lopez gets up early six days a week to open up the small *bodega* (store) she runs in Saucillo, a village in the state of Chihuahua in northern Mexico. ²Señora Lopez stocks a limited number of items for her customers. ³She sells some products that require refrigeration, such as milk, eggs, meats, and vegetables, as well as staples like flour, salt, sugar, and canned goods.

⁴Most of Maria's customers work in a nearby oil refinery or are farmers. ⁵To help feed their families, many grow some of their own food and raise animals. ⁶Maria calls nearly all her customers by their first names and always attends their christenings, weddings, and funerals. ⁷She saves the freshest produce and best cuts of meat for her favorite customers and even keeps up with their diets.

⁸Tony Lopez, Maria's third cousin, manages a large Kroger supermarket on the west side of San Antonio, Texas. . . . ⁹Tony tries to spend at least an hour a day on the shopping floor chatting with customers and employees. ¹⁰But most of his time is taken up meeting with route salespeople for various grocery distributors and checking with Kroger's regional buyers.

¹¹Keeping such a mammoth store fully stocked requires careful planning, buying, and coordinating. ¹²Each morning, a computer printout from Kroger's regional office in San Antonio tells Tony the previous day's sales. ¹³It also provides a great deal more information: how many quarts of milk, crates of grapefruit, boxes of Tide (in each size), and packages of Green Giant frozen peas were sold.

_____ 1. Although Maria Lopez and Tony Lopez get their information in different ways, both are well-informed about their customers' needs and tastes.

_____ 2. Like Maria, Tony probably calls most of his customers by their first names.

_____ 3. Maria Lopez is more a part of her customers' lives than Tony Lopez is of his.

_____ 4. Despite the differences in their stores, Maria and Tony probably earn very similar incomes.

_____ 5. We can assume that a smaller percentage of Tony's customers grow vegetables or raise animals than the percentage of Maria's customers who do.

_____ 6. A computerized analysis of stock would be as useful for Maria's work as it is to Tony's.

_____ 7. Unlike Tony's store, Maria's store is not part of a supermarket chain.

_____ 8. The differences between Maria's and Tony's stores are closely tied to the differences between the communities they serve.

_____ 9. Since Tony has a much larger and more modern store to work in, he must enjoy his work a lot more than Maria does.

_____ 10. The Kroger customers expect less of a personal relationship with their store's manager than the *bodega*'s customers do.

INFERENCES: Test D

A. (1–6.) Read the following textbook passage, and then check the **six** statements which are most logically supported by the information given.

[1]Some behavioral psychologists have suggested that the personality could be precisely molded by training. [2]However, research now indicates that a child's temperament is probably predetermined, at least to some extent. [3]That is not to say that parents cannot guide and advise their children and help them to achieve a sense of self-worth. [4]For instance, setting limits for an aggressive child or gently urging a shy one to try new experiences could help youngsters to realize their full potential. [5]But trying to force a child to fit a particular model would probably be counterproductive.

[6]One therapist advises against attempts to radically redesign the personality. [7]Rather, he quotes a rabbi to illustrate the wisdom of trying to develop what is uniquely oneself. [8]The rabbi said that when he reached the kingdom of God, he knew he would not be asked, "Why weren't you Moses? Why weren't you David?" but "Why weren't you fully yourself?"

_____ 1. The author feels that parental guidance is not important.

_____ 2. The passage suggests that with guidance, a very shy child can become at least a little more outgoing.

_____ 3. In the past, behavioral psychologists have believed that the personality could be significantly changed.

_____ 4. Personality is determined by a child's environment, not his genes.

_____ 5. Genetic makeup has a great deal to do with personality.

_____ 6. The author suggests that personality is determined only by genetic makeup.

_____ 7. The rabbi probably believed that everyone has a unique contribution to make to society.

_____ 8. The author would probably agree with the idea that anyone can be a great artist, politician, or religious leader.

_____ 9. The passage suggests that it's better not to judge yourself in comparison to others.

_____ 10. The passage suggests that it is wise to be accepting of your child's fundamental temperament and interests.

(Continues on next page)

B. (7–10.) Read the following passage from *The Language of Clothes* by writer and educator Alison Lurie, and then check the **four** statements which are most logically supported by the information given.

banal: dull or commonplace

[1]In the past, sexual modesty was often proposed as the purpose of dress. [2]The Bible tells us that this was the original reason for wearing clothes: Adam and Eve, once they realized that they were naked, "sewed fig leaves together, and made themselves aprons." [3]Historically, however, shame seems to have played very little part in the development of costume. [4]In ancient Egypt, Crete and Greece, the naked body was not considered immodest; slaves and athletes habitually went without clothing, while people of high rank wore garments that were cut and draped so as to show a good deal when in motion.

[5]Some modern writers believe that the deliberate concealment of certain parts of the body originated not as a way of discouraging sexual interest, but as a clever device for arousing it. [6]According to this view, clothes are the physical equivalent of remarks like "I've got a secret"; they are a tease, a come-on. [7]It is certainly true that parts of the human form considered sexually arousing are often covered in such a way as to exaggerate and draw attention to them. [8]People done up in shiny colored wrappings and bows affect us just as a birthday present does: we're curious, turned on; we want to undo the package. . . .

[9]Many visitors to nudist camps report that the sight of all that uncovered flesh brings fatigue and a sense of being slightly unwell. [10]Later, after one gets used to it, as the ancients were, it seems merely banal.

_____ 1. All cultures have agreed on the purpose of dress.

_____ 2. The author obviously feels that people should not dress in sexually arousing ways.

_____ 3. In ancient Egypt, Crete, and Greece, people showed more of their bodies than most Americans do today.

_____ 4. The author feels that nudist camps should not be allowed.

_____ 5. In ancient Egypt, Crete, and Greece, athletes were slaves.

_____ 6. From the passage we can conclude that clothing must have been very expensive in ancient Egypt, Crete, and Greece.

_____ 7. In a society without clothing, the naked body is not particularly thrilling.

_____ 8. The passage suggests that nudity in nudist camps generally leads to loose sexual behavior.

_____ 9. We might conclude from the passage that a tight dress can be more sexy to some than a topless bathing suit.

_____ 10. Behavior we consider basic may not be basic to other cultures.

PURPOSE AND TONE: Test A

A. In the space provided, indicate whether the primary purpose of each sentence is to inform (**I**), to persuade (**P**), or to entertain (**E**).

_____ 1. If you spend a dollar every minute, it will take you about twenty centuries to spend a billion dollars.

_____ 2. By selling candy and other junk food in the lunchroom, public schools are teaching poor nutrition; such "lessons" should not be allowed.

_____ 3. I asked my boss for a raise, so he moved my office from the basement to the second floor.

_____ 4 People should not be allowed to have children until they take a parenting class.

_____ 5. Between 93 and 95 percent of all fertile married couples choose to have children.

_____ 6. Insanity is hereditary. You get it from your kids.

_____ 7. Have your eyes checked at the We Care Eye Care Center, where we sell glasses at a discount to families.

B. Each of the following passages illustrates one of the tones named in the box below. In each space provided, write the letter of the tone that applies to the passage. Two tone choices will be left over.

A. ironic	B. annoyed	C. enthusiastic
D. distressed	E. forgiving	

_____ 8. [1]Strawberries are now available in the markets, and what a winning crop! [2]In contrast to last year's berries, which were badly affected by poor weather conditions, these are plentiful, delicious, and relatively inexpensive. [3]They will make a fine climax to any meal, whether under a dollop of sour cream laced with brown sugar or crushed over a scoop of vanilla ice cream. [4]In fact, these luscious berries are so sweet, they can stand very well on their own. [5]Strawberry lovers won't be disappointed.

_____ 9. [1]I visited my grandmother in a nursing home yesterday. [2]Ninety-two years old and partially paralyzed by a stroke, she now struggles to feed herself and is irreversibly bound to her bed or wheelchair. [3]Once vital and fiercely independent, she is now frail and incapable of even using the bathroom unassisted. [4]Mortified by her dependence on others, her moods range from quiet acceptance to whining complaint. [5]I do not see evidence of a divine plan in this situation. [6]Maybe there is no divine plan, or perhaps I am just not wise enough to see it.

(Continues on next page)

_____ 10. [1]Eighth-grader Terry met his friend Ron in front of Ron's house on the first day of summer vacation. [2]Ron looked at Terry's broad grin and remarked sympathetically, "I can't help but notice that you look utterly miserable. [3]You can confide in me—what's the matter?"

[4]Still smiling, Terry sighed and replied, "Well, who wouldn't be bummed out, confronted as we are with weeks stretching in front of us and nothing to do but waste the most beautiful months of the year on unimportant pursuits like basketball, fishing, and bike riding."

[5]"Yeah," whined Ron, as the two ambled towards the nearby basketball court. [6]"And the most depressing thing of all is that we don't get to see our valued colleague, Mr. Petersham, in the principal's office all summer."

[7]"We must try to endure it with superior courage," Terry replied, and then he dashed onto the court for his first lay-up.

(Note: Select the tone that describes the boys' conversation.)

PURPOSE AND TONE: Test B

A. Eight quotations in the story below are preceded by a blank space. Identify the tone of each italicized quotation by writing in the letter of one of these tones. (Two tone choices will be left over.)

A. bewildered	B. calming	C. critical
D. grateful	E. matter-of-fact	F. pessimistic
G. praising	H. remorseful	I. sorrowful
J. threatening		

Tryouts for *The Wizard of Oz* were held Wednesday afternoon. The first student read for the part of Dorothy, the little girl who is swept away, along with her dog Toto, to the land of Oz.

_____ 1. *"Toto!"* she read. *"Where are we? Everything looks so strange! I don't think we're in Kansas anymore!"*

_____ 2. *"Very nice!"* said the teacher. *"You sound as if you've acted before!"*

Another student stepped up to read the lines of the Wicked Witch of the West.

_____ 3. *"Just try to stay out of my way!"* the "witch" hissed at Dorothy. *"I'm going to get you, the ruby slippers, and your nasty little dog, too!"*

Next a student tried out for the part of the Tin Woodman, who wanted a heart more than anything.

_____ 4. *"I'm just an empty kettle,"* he said with a sob. *"I am a heart-less piece of metal."*

While some students were reading for parts, others stood in the back of the room, whispering among themselves.

_____ 5. *"That last guy who read for the Cowardly Lion was really terrible,"* said one student.

_____ 6. *"I thought I'd try out for the part of Dorothy,"* a girl said, *"but I probably wouldn't have a chance. I never win anything."*

After all the students who wanted to read had their chance, the drama teacher spoke to them once more before they left the room.

_____ 7. *"Thank you all for coming. I really appreciate your interest in the drama department activities,"* she said with a warm smile.

_____ 8. As they began to leave, she added, *"My choices for the parts will be posted on the bulletin boards Friday morning."*

(Continues on next page)

B. In the space provided, indicate whether the primary purpose of each passage is to inform (**I**), to persuade (**P**), or to entertain (**E**).

_____ 9. [1]Until recently, it was commonly believed by intelligence experts that people reach the height of their intellectual peak by the time they're twenty. [2]Lately, however, scientists have discovered that our minds continue to grow long after we are fully developed physically. [3]In addition, some psychologists are expanding their notion of what makes up intelligence. [4]Dr. Robert Sternberg of Yale University, for example, outlines seven different areas of intelligence, including musical ability and self-knowledge.

_____ 10. [1]Cats are allowed to roam just about wherever they please (try and stop them), and even dogs have the run of the house, or at least of a portion of the house. [2]But pet birds are generally limited for most of their lives to the space defined by the four sides of a small cage. [3]Yet birds are born to flap and swoop through wide spaces of sky, unlimited neither by walls nor ceilings. [4]To keep a creature born with wings in a small space, unable to use its major natural means of transportation, is unfair. [5]People who want birds as pets should at least find ways to allow the birds to fly freely within one or two rooms of the house.

PURPOSE AND TONE: Test C

Read each of the paragraphs below. Then carefully consider the questions that follow and write the letters of the best responses.

A. [1]Single, divorced, or widowed adults usually live either alone or with other family members. [2]The idea of two unmarried adults joining forces in one household is one that has been too little explored in our society. [3]When two divorced mothers and their children live together, everyone benefits. [4]The adults can offer each other emotional support and practical assistance that isn't available in a single-parent household. [5]The arrangement has similar advantages for unmarried or widowed persons. [6]They can share expenses and household tasks while providing companionship for one another. [7]Our commission should encourage such relationships by setting up a clearinghouse in which people can seek housing partnerships.

____ 1. The primary purpose of this paragraph is to
   A. inform.
   B. persuade.
   C. entertain.

____ 2. The tone of this paragraph is
   A. disappointed and hurt.
   B. disbelieving and uncertain.
   C. straightforward and caring.
   D. pessimistic and pleading.

B. [1]I can't thank Rob and Elsie sincerely enough for introducing me to Sheila. [2]They promised me she was exactly my type, and how accurate they were—I've been yearning for a vain, shallow woman with the IQ of a turnip. [3]Sheila and I hit it off immediately. [4]When I picked her up in my Ford Escort, she wrinkled her adorable nose with exasperation and said, "I thought Elsie said you had a decent car." [5]I took her to eat at Luigi's and was thrilled by the way she sneered and said, "You are a cheapskate, aren't you?" [6]When I suggested we see a foreign film and she announced that she never sees anything with subtitles because she hates to read, I wanted to marry her on the spot. [7]I'll certainly have to think of some way to repay my dear friends for fixing me up with such a marvelous girl.

____ 3. The purpose of this paragraph is to
   A. explain that the date with Sheila was a mistake.
   B. argue against blind dates.
   C. both of the above.

____ 4. The tone of this paragraph is
   A. uncertain but grateful.
   B. angry and bewildered.
   C. understanding and forgiving.
   D. ironic and mocking.

(Continues on next page)

C. ¹Many adult Americans, particularly males, do not have especially close friends. ²This is unfortunate for a number of reasons. ³The lack of close friends places an unrealistic burden on a person's spouse. ⁴He or she is expected to provide all the other's emotional needs. ⁵In addition, without close friends, adults become emotionally limited. ⁶They lose the ability to express themselves freely to other people. ⁷The Bangwa tribe of Western Africa, by contrast, value friendship so highly that parents assign each of their children a "best friend" in infancy. ⁸Friends spend a great deal of time together throughout their lives. ⁹The worst part of being old, complained one elderly Bangwa man, was that he had no best friend left to gossip with.

___ 5. The primary purpose of this paragraph is to
    A. present facts about adult friendship.
    B. argue that adult friendship is valuable.
    C. entertain with amusing customs of other cultures.

___ 6. The tone of the paragraph is
    A. excited.
    B. straightforward.
    C. fearful.
    D. disbelieving.

D. ¹"Secret Medical Breakthrough!" screams the headline. ²"Melt Pounds Away While You Sleep!" ³Then there's "The Cure For AIDS Is Right In Your Refrigerator!" ⁴Or how about "Swiss Scientists Promise: You'll Never Have Another Cold!" ⁵Advertisements and "news" stories like these appear in every supermarket tabloid and in the back pages of innumerable other publications. ⁶They all seem based on the same doubtful premise: "Doctors don't want you to know the truth, but we're going to tell you anyway." ⁷Don't let tabloid headlines tempt you into spending your hard-earned money. ⁸The gullible readers who swallow these claims never seem to stop and ask why, if these stories of amazing cures and sure-fire remedies are true, they haven't made headlines in newspapers and other publications. ⁹An AIDS cure? ¹⁰A genuine weight-loss plan that involves no dieting or exercising? ¹¹If such stories were true, you wouldn't be reading about them first in the supermarket checkout aisle. ¹²If the public stopped supporting these publications, they would no longer be able to falsely raise hopes for thousands of readers.

___ 7. The primary purpose of this paragraph is to
    A. explain the difference between tabloids and other newspapers.
    B. persuade readers not to support tabloids.
    C. tell amusing facts about tabloids.

___ 8. The overall tone of the paragraph is
    A. critical.
    B. uncertain.
    C. depressed.
    D. lighthearted.

PURPOSE AND TONE: Test D

Read each of the paragraphs below. Then carefully consider the questions that follow and write the letters of the best responses.

A. [1]Consumers may be influenced to buy an item not only by its price and quality, but also by the image it projects—and the image may be just that, only an image. [2]For instance, consider the cases of Haägen-Dazs ice cream and its competitor, Frusen Glådje. [3]Both are rich "gourmet" ice creams, and both cost considerably more than most other supermarket brands. [4]Both appeal to the consumer through their Scandinavian-sounding names, which imply that they are imported and thus superior or special in some way. [5]The Haägen-Dazs package even shows a map of Norway and Denmark, further suggesting a Scandinavian connection. [6]But that special "imported" quality is wholly in the mind of the consumer: Haägen-Dazs is manufactured in New Jersey, and Frusen Glådje in Philadelphia.

____ 1. The primary purpose of this paragraph is to
    A. inform.
    B. persuade.
    C. entertain.

____ 2. The tone of the paragraph can be described as
    A. mainly matter-of-fact.
    B. largely optimistic.
    C. greatly amused.
    D. very angry.

B. [1]Our world is paying a stiff price for chronic air pollution. [2]If dramatic changes are not made, pollutants will continue to rob us of money and health. [3]They damage buildings and automobiles. [4]Crops, livestock, roads, and metals are all hurt by air pollution. [5]We must pay millions to clean everything from soot-blackened buildings to curtains dirtied with pollutants. [6]If nothing else can persuade us to cut down on air pollution, perhaps the threats to our health will. [7]Our bodies are paying the highest price of all for living in a polluted land. [8]Breathing the air in New York City is equivalent to smoking several packs of cigarettes a day. [9]The poisons in the air accumulate in our bodies, leading to bronchitis, emphysema, and lung cancer.

____ 3. The primary purpose of this paragraph is to
    A. inform readers of facts about air pollution.
    B. persuade readers that air pollution must be reduced.
    C. amuse readers with details of ridiculous human error.

____ 4. The tone of this paragraph can be described as
    A. arrogantly sarcastic.
    B. sympathetic but angry.
    C. greatly concerned.
    D. bitterly revengeful.

(Continues on next page)

C. [1]I've been noticing a lot of cat-related items for sale recently: cat calendars, cat wallpaper, cat coffee mugs. [2]These I cannot comprehend—cats are meant to be companions, not interior decorations. [3]Worse are the cat psychology books, those with titles like *You Can Toilet Train Your Cat!* and *Command Your Cat to Sit, Stay, Lie Down!* [4]First, I don't believe any of this is possible. [5]I know when I suggest to my cat that he do anything other than lie in the sun, eat, and accept the adoration of humans, he gives me a cold stare that invites me to have my head examined. [6]Second, I've always felt that much of a cat's charm lies in his refusal to cooperate with anyone's silly ideas about "training" him. [7]If you want an animal to sit, stay, and lie down on command, get a German shepherd.

____ 5. The primary purpose of this paragraph is to
    A. seriously inform readers about cat-related products and books.
    B. persuade readers not to buy such products or books.
    C. entertain readers with observations about such products and books.

____ 6. The overall tone of this paragraph can be described as
    A. sarcastic and anxious.
    B. caring and forgiving.
    C. playful and humorous.
    D. regretful and surprised.

D. [1]You may think that buttons near the lower edge of jacket sleeves are just there for looks. [2]That may be so today, but buttons on sleeves originally had a more practical purpose. [3]During the frigid winter of 1812, Napoleon and his troops invaded Russia. [4]As might be expected, many of his soldiers had runny noses from colds and flu, and—to put it delicately—they didn't have the neatest habits for dealing with this problem. [5]This disturbed Napoleon, who was known to hate sloppiness and poor manners, so he instructed the military tailors to add metal buttons to the sleeves of his soldiers' jackets. [6]Have you ever tried to wipe your nose on ice-cold buttons?

____ 7. The primary purpose of this paragraph is to
    A. inform readers about the unusual original purpose of buttons on sleeves.
    B. persuade readers to buy jackets with buttons on the sleeves.
    C. tell a joke.

____ 8. The tone of the paragraph can be described as
    A. ironic and humorous.
    B. loving and slightly sentimental.
    C. straightforward and somewhat amused.
    D. formal but passionate and outspoken.

ARGUMENT: Test A

A. (1–4.) In each group, one statement is the point of an argument, and the other statements are support for that point. Write the letter of the point of each group.

___ *Group 1*

   A. Curved streets discourage speeding cars.

   B. For residential neighborhoods, curved streets have advantages.

   C. The graceful lines of curved streets are more attractive than straight lines.

___ *Group 2*

   A. In stores, at bus stops, and at theaters, people are expected to wait for their turn in line.

   B. In cities, many everyday activities occur according to a system of rules.

   C. In North America, pedestrians keep to the right as a way to avoid running into others.

   D. Drivers are expected to stick to one side of the road.

___ *Group 3*

   A. In recent years, 62 percent of all traffic deaths took place at night.

   B. The chances of being in a fatal accident are nearly four times greater at night than during the day.

   C. Driving at night is less safe than driving in the daytime.

   D. Many dangerous corners and curves are poorly lit or unlit at night.

___ *Group 4*

   A. Dinosaur fossils teach us about animals that are now extinct.

   B. Fossils have "recorded" much about the past of the Earth and its inhabitants.

   C. Fossils of ferns found in the Arctic suggest climatic changes.

   D. Seashell fossils found high in the mountains indicate that those areas were once covered by salt water.

B. Each point is followed by three statements that provide relevant support and three that do not. In the spaces, write the letters of the **three** relevant statements of support.

Point: Selling cigarettes ought to be against the law.

   A. Cigarette smoking kills many more people than all illegal drugs combined.

   B. Today, tobacco growing is actually supported by government subsidies.

   C. Smoking makes clothing smell bad and stains teeth.

   D. Alcohol is another legal drug that kills numerous Americans every year.

   E. Nonsmokers are endangered by breathing the smoke from others' cigarettes.

   F. Tobacco is one of the most addictive of all drugs.

   5–7. *Items that logically support the point:* _____ _____ _____

(Continues on next page)

Point: Taking good care of a pet is healthy for the pet owner.

    A. Before-and-after studies have shown that petting an animal causes a decrease in many people's blood pressure.

    B. Owning a dog that needs a daily walk can encourage a senior citizen to get some much-needed exercise.

    C. Most people can easily afford the expense of pet food and veterinary care.

    D. According to the 2007–2008 National Pet Owners Survey, 63 percent of American households own a pet.

    E. The American Heart Association has said that pet owners are more likely to survive during the first year after a heart attack than people who don't own pets.

    F. In addition to cats and dogs, people have fish, birds, snakes, pigs, and even insects for pets.

8–10. *Items that logically support the point:* _____ _____ _____

ARGUMENT: Test B

A. Write the letter of the sentence that does **not** support the point of the argument in each paragraph.

¹Getting rid of the eyesores in a neighborhood does more than simply beautify; it can improve the economic and social life of an area. ²Not long ago, a neighborhood in Philadelphia decided to improve its appearance by planting a community garden and installing trash cans. ³As a result, neighbors spent more time together outdoors. ⁴Thus graffiti writers and more serious offenders were discouraged from frequenting the area. ⁵The cleaner streets and safer atmosphere also attracted more customers to local businesses. ⁶Additional police on the streets also keep streets safer.

____ 1. Which sentence does **not** support the author's conclusion that getting rid of community eyesores can improve the local economic and social life?
  A. Sentence 3
  B. Sentence 4
  C. Sentence 5
  D. Sentence 6

¹Some people argue that music videos have hurt popular music by emphasizing looks rather than the music itself. ²In fact, though, what music videos have done is bring new attention to another art form: dance. ³Today, talented dancers can become top-name entertainers after being showcased by music videos. ⁴Pop star Paula Abdul, for example, gained fame as a choreographer and dancer in music videos. ⁵Ten or twenty years ago, dancers had far fewer opportunities to become known. ⁶The music video industry has also created hundreds of new job opportunities for video producers, directors, and technicians. ⁷Thanks to videos, dance is showcased in a way not seen since the days of song-and-dance musicals in the 1940s and 1950s.

____ 2. Which sentence does **not** support the author's conclusion that music videos have brought new attention to dance?
  A. Sentence 3
  B. Sentence 5
  C. Sentence 6
  D. Sentence 7

¹Be sure to include organic food in your supermarket basket. ²First of all, eating organic produce may be good for you. ³Nonorganic fruits, vegetables and grains are sprayed with pesticides; some of them, such as strawberries, are treated with a great deal of pesticides. ⁴And some scientists believe that consuming pesticides over many years may turn out to cause cancer or other diseases. ⁵In fact, some farmers are beginning to notice that they are getting sick themselves from using so many pesticides. ⁶Also, organic food is becoming more and more popular. ⁷Furthermore,

(Continues on next page)

organic farmers tend to build up and enrich the soil better than nonorganic farmers do. [8]Their methods are not only better for the Earth; they tend to produce better tasting fruits and vegetables.

_____ 3. Which of the following sentences does **not** support the author's argument that it's a good idea to buy organic food?
   A. Sentence 2
   B. Sentence 6
   C. Sentence 7
   D. Sentence 8

B. For each group, read the three items of support (the evidence). Then write the letter of the point that is adequately supported by that evidence.

Group 1

Support:

   • Janis Chavez served three terms on the city council.
   • Ms. Chavez was head of the local planning commission for several years.
   • She has also served as a special assistant to the mayor.

_____ 4. Which of the following conclusions is best supported by the evidence above?
   A. Janis Chavez is the best qualified candidate for mayor.
   B. Janis Chavez has devoted her entire life to public service.
   C. Janis Chavez has always worked for the voters' best interests.
   D. Janis Chavez has broad experience in city government.

Group 2

Support:

   • Stevie Wonder, a blind pianist, singer and composer, won over 20 Grammy Awards, including an "Album of the Year" award for *Songs in the Key of Life*.
   • Franklin Delano Roosevelt, the popular U.S. president who was elected for four terms, was paralyzed by polio.
   • Beethoven, one of the greatest musical composers who ever lived, was completely deaf in his later years—even when he wrote and conducted his famous Ninth Symphony.

_____ 5. Which of the following conclusions is best supported by the evidence above?
   A. Disabled people are more likely than others to achieve success in the field of music.
   B. Individuals with disabilities can achieve greatness.
   C. Disabled people become more famous than equally talented people who aren't disabled.
   D. People with disabilities aren't given enough opportunities to contribute to society.

ARGUMENT: Test C

A. Each of the two points below is followed by six items, three of which logically support the point and three of which do not. In the spaces provided, write the letters of the **three** items that logically support each point.

Point: Boxing should be banned.

A. Promoters make a great deal of money.

B. Boxers have died from injuries received in the ring.

C. The sport of boxing began in ancient Greece.

D. The main point of boxing is for opponents to badly hurt each other.

E. Only a handful of boxers are very successful.

F. Boxers have been permanently brain-damaged from the constant blows to the head.

1–3. *Items that logically support the point:* _____ _____ _____

Point: Sometimes the "newest thing" is something old that has made a comeback.

A. Some cities that tore out their streetcar lines years ago are now putting them back.

B. The basic black dress has never really gone out of fashion.

C. Miniskirts, a 1960s fashion, became popular again in the 1980s.

D. Fashions are more varied today than ever before.

E. Many recent buildings have a 1930s look to them.

F. The work of architect and designer Frank Lloyd Wright is still admired today.

4–6. *Items that logically support the point:* _____ _____ _____

B. Read the following three items of support (the evidence). Then write the letter of the point that is adequately supported by that evidence.

Support:

• Many sports teams are named for Native American tribes or features of Indian cultures.

• *Dances with Wolves*, a film sympathetic to Native Americans, was one of the hit movies of 1990.

• The Indian peoples' reverence for nature has become a model for a new environmental ethic.

____ 7. Which of the following conclusions is best supported by the evidence above?

A. Many cars have been named for Native American tribes.

B. Native Americans have fewer social problems than in previous times.

C. Native Americans have influenced the general culture of the country.

D. Native Americans are greater sports fans than other Americans.

(Continues on next page)

C. Read the paragraphs below, and then write the letter of the best answer to each question that follows.

[1]To have a successful budget, it is useful to include a category called "miscellaneous." [2]It is hard to remember every single item you buy. [3]And supermarket impulse purchases, such as gum and magazines, can result in a busted budget. [4]Certain supermarket purchases—such as candy—are best omitted from a health standpoint as well. [5]Extra gas for an unscheduled trip that requires spending beyond the usual fuel allowance can also ruin your spending plan. [6]You can even get in the red by buying ice cream cones at the dairy stand if they're not provided for under the food or entertainment categories. [7]Keeping track of these various expenses for several months will reveal an amount that is suitable to include under "miscellaneous."

____ 8. Which sentence is **not** relevant to the author's argument that a miscellaneous category can help you have a successful budget?
   A. Sentence 3
   B. Sentence 4
   C. Sentence 5
   D. Sentence 6

[1]The annual highway death rate has dropped 40 percent since the late 1970s primarily because of the safety features now available in vehicles. [2]Seat belts automatically present themselves, encouraging drivers and passengers to use them. [3]Air bags inflate instantly during impact, preventing deaths in many circumstances. [4]Anti-lock brakes often allow drivers to avoid an accident because the car can stop in a shorter distance with greater control. [5]Campaigns against drunk driving may also be making a dent in traffic accidents. [6]And fog lights improve visibility for the driver and make it easier for oncoming drivers to see the vehicle.

____ 9. Which statement is the point of the argument?
   A. More safety features should be built into vehicles.
   B. The safety features now available on vehicles are saving lives.
   C. For too many years, automotive manufacturing companies resisted useful safety features.
   D. One of the most important safety features on vehicles is the anti-lock brakes.

____ 10. Which statement is **not** relevant to the point of the argument?
   A. Sentence 2
   B. Sentence 3
   C. Sentence 5
   D. Sentence 6

ARGUMENT: Test D

A. The point below is followed by six items, three of which logically support the point and three of which do not. In the spaces provided, write the letters of the **three** items that logically support each point.

Point: Hypnosis can be a useful tool in various medical situations.
  A. Many medical professionals feel that hypnosis is nothing more than a form of entertainment.
  B. Hemophiliacs typically bleed so much from dental treatment that they need to be given several pints of blood, but some who were hypnotized during treatment needed no blood at all.
  C. People who are especially susceptible to hypnosis are often fantasy-prone.
  D. Suggestions given under hypnosis have improved headaches, asthma, and warts.
  E. Hypnosis has been found to be more effective than morphine in alleviating certain types of pain.
  F. People can be hypnotized to do something after they are brought out from a state of hypnosis.

  1–3. *Items that logically support the point:*   _____   _____   _____

Point: The blood system is the distribution network of the body.
  A. The blood system carries food and oxygen to all the body's cells.
  B. The human body has about six quarts of blood.
  C. Circulating blood delivers hormones throughout the body.
  D. A decrease in the number of circulating red blood cells is called anemia.
  E. In an emergency, the liquid inside young coconuts can be used for blood transfusions.
  F. The blood system collects the body's wastes and brings them to the organs which remove them.

  4–6. *Items that logically support the point:*   _____   _____   _____

B. Read the following three items of support (the evidence). Then write the letter of the point that is adequately supported by that evidence.

Support:
  • By 1860 (just before the Civil War began), one person out of every four in the U.S. lived in a city.
  • By 1890, one out of every three people in the U.S. lived in a city.
  • Half of all the people living in the U.S. in 1910 lived in a city.

____ 7. Which of the following conclusions is best supported by the evidence above?
  A. At the end of the 1800s and the beginning of the 1900s, there was a strong movement of people to the cities.

(Continues on next page)

B. In the years following the Civil War, people felt safer living in a city.

C. By the early part of the twentieth century, people no longer wished to settle in the West.

D. Since 1910, numerous people have gone back to rural America.

C. Read the paragraphs below, and then answer the questions that follow.

[1]Individual and family stress would be lessened and family togetherness increased if household responsibilities were assigned more evenly among family members. [2]Often wives who work full-time also do most of the work around the house, which makes their lives more stressful than necessary. [3]This stress often causes wives to resent their husbands and children, creating tensions throughout the family. [4]America's husbands have always been too self-centered. [5]A more fair distribution of household work would also free wives to spend more relaxing time together with their families. [6]If household work was more fairly divided, everyone's lives would undoubtedly be improved.

____ 8. Which sentence is **not** relevant to the author's argument that assigning household responsibilities more evenly would lessen stress and increase togetherness?
   A. Sentence 2
   B. Sentence 3
   C. Sentence 4
   D. Sentence 5

[1]Forty-six out of ninety-three bottles of various brands of water tested in a major study had detectable levels of potentially harmful chemicals. [2]The levels didn't exceed Environmental Protection Agency limits—but, then, neither do those of tap water from urban areas with municipal water-treatment plants. [3]Indeed, it was found that most tap water can be as pure as—or purer than—some bottled waters. [4]And many taste just as good too. [5]It was also noted that tap water has as many "healthy" minerals as bottled water. [6]"The minerals in tap and bottled water are comparable, and vary only slightly," noted one dietician involved in the study. [7]Obviously, tap water can be as healthy as or healthier than bottled water.

____ 9. Which sentence expresses the point of the argument?
   A. Sentence 1
   B. Sentence 2
   C. Sentence 5
   D. Sentence 7

____10. Which sentence is **not** relevant support for the point of the argument?
   A. Sentence 2
   B. Sentence 3
   C. Sentence 4
   D. Sentence 6

CRITICAL READING: Test A (Fact and Opinion)

A. Two of the statements below are facts, and three are opinions. In addition, **two** statements include both fact and opinion. Identify facts with an **F**, opinions with an **O**, and statements of fact *and* opinion with **F+O**.

_____ 1. Couples should know each other for at least a year before getting married.

_____ 2. For various reasons, some spouses take separate vacations.

_____ 3. In point of fact, it is always better for spouses to vacation together.

_____ 4. Here's a disgusting fact: By the time the average person is 70, he or she will have shed about forty pounds of dead skin.

_____ 5. Some human eyes are so sensitive that on a clear, dark night they can spot a candle flame more than thirty miles away.

_____ 6. Paul Revere is famous for his midnight ride to warn the colonists that the British were coming during the American Revolution, but he should be equally honored for his fine work as a silversmith.

_____ 7. No reform movement of any era was more significant than the drive to abolish slavery.

B. (8–10.) The following paragraph contains three sentences. One is fact, one is opinion, and one sentence combines fact and opinion. Identify the fact with an **F**, the opinion with an **O**, and the statement of fact *and* opinion with an **F+O**.

[1]People who think of Alaska as an unattractive frozen wasteland are just plain wrong. [2]Alaska is a land of various wildlife, varying climates, and hundreds of forms of plant life. [3]In fact, the highest mountains in North America are in Alaska, where they have a starring role in some unforgettable scenery.

8. _____   9. _____   10. _____

C. (11–15.) The passage below contains five sentences. Each sentence expresses a fact, the author's opinion, or a combination of fact and opinion. Identify each sentence as fact (**F**), opinion (**O**), or fact *and* opinion (**F+O**).

[1]Red is the most common color for barns throughout the United States. [2]It's fortunate that red is such a good color for barns because the early farmers who established the tradition didn't have other paint colors to choose from. [3]Pioneer farmers painted their barns with a mixture of skim milk, linseed oil, lime, and iron oxide, with the iron oxide furnishing the red color to the mixture. [4]Since outdoor paints are now available in a variety of colors, today's farmers paint their barns red out of choice, not necessity. [5]Everyone of taste would certainly agree that the countryside would be less beautiful if it were dotted with, for example, jet-black, purple or ultramarine barns.

11. _____   12. _____   13. _____   14. _____   15. _____

(Continues on next page)

D. Read the following passage from an article in *Fortune* magazine, and then identify each of the listed excerpts from the passage as fact (**F**), the author's opinion (**O**), or a combination of fact *and* opinion (**F+O**). (Only one of the excerpts combines fact and opinion.)

¹There was plenty of gossip in the corridors of Levi Strauss when Donna Goya, a personnel manager and rising star, cut back to a three-day-a-week work schedule. ²"One of my colleagues thanked me for taking myself out of the running," she recalls. ³Two years later, with her son in kindergarten, Goya returned to regular hours—and a promotion to director of personnel. ⁴The colleague who was glad to see her leave? ⁵"Now he works for me."

⁶Donna Goya belongs to a pioneering group of managers and professionals who are breaking the stranglehold of the five-day workweek to devote more time to other aspects of their lives, such as caring for a young child or an elderly parent. ⁷These men and women have told their companies that, for a while, they will require flexible work schedules. ⁸The surprise is that, in many cases, their careers are prospering. ⁹It's still an uphill battle against well-established corporate practice, but by now enough companies have tried this kind of new approach that some lessons can be learned. ¹⁰And they ought to be.

¹¹*Flexible* is a term that covers a variety of arrangements: hours other than nine to five, part-time work, job sharing, leaves of absence, working at home. ¹²From the company's perspective, the theory goes, allowing employees to work fewer and more flexible hours is a powerful way to attract and retain top-caliber people. ¹³Adaptable schedules should also promote a sense of empowerment among workers and a feeling that the company trusts them. ¹⁴Most important, these work arrangements enable dual-career parents to address the serious societal issue of raising children responsibly.

¹⁵Sounds great. ¹⁶Why is it, then, that employees even of seemingly progressive companies still encounter a lot of resistance when they try to take advantage of the option? . . .

¹⁷Now some of the most forward-looking corporations—among them American Express, IBM, Levi Strauss, NCNB, and PepsiCo—are systematically trying to promote flexibility throughout their organizations.

_____ 16. Two years later, with her son in kindergarten, Goya returned to regular hours—and a promotion to director of personnel.

_____ 17. These men and women have told their companies that, for a while, they will require flexible work schedules.

_____ 18. And they ought to be.

_____ 19. *Flexible* is a term that covers a variety of arrangements: hours other than nine to five, part-time work, job sharing, leaves of absence, working at home.

_____ 20. Now some of the most forward-looking corporations—among them American Express, IBM, Levi Strauss, NCNB, and PepsiCo—are systematically trying to promote flexibility throughout their organizations.

CRITICAL READING: Test B

A. Each pair of items below illustrates a particular propaganda technique. On the line next to each pair, write the letter of the main technique being used.

_____ 1. • An Olympic gold medalist who suffers from asthma recommends the Medco pharmacy program.

• The governor of California appears in a political ad on television saying that people should vote for Bob Green for state representative.

    A. Glittering generalities   C. Transfer
    B. Testimonial   D. Bandwagon

_____ 2. • A laundry care product proclaims that "A fresh touch of goodness makes life wonderful."

• A theme park advertises: "Where the Magic Begins!"

    A. Testimonial   C. Transfer
    B. Glittering generalities D. Name calling

_____ 3. • A magazine ad shows a picture of a beautiful young model in a bikini. She is lying on the beach with a can of diet soda beside her.

• A Ford Motor Company ad shows three of its SUVs driving up a steep, rocky mountain trail. Beneath the picture is the caption: "The Ford Escape! The Ford Explorer! The Ford Expedition!"

    A. Name calling   C. Bandwagon
    B. Plain folks   D. Transfer

_____ 4. • A radio ad tells us, "Good Neighbor Pharmacies are locally owned and operated. Your pharmacist lives and works in your own neighborhood."

• Television news shows the vice president of the United States in an army mess hall. He is serving Thanksgiving dinners to soldiers.

    A. Transfer   C. Plain folks
    B. Glittering generalities D. Testimonial

_____ 5. • A candidate for the United States Senate stands on the steps of the Lincoln Memorial as he announces his candidacy.

• A television ad for ChemLawn shows an attractive young mother and two young children happily playing on a lush green lawn.

    A. Testimonial   C. Transfer
    B. Bandwagon   D. Name calling

(Continues on next page)

_____ 6. • Try Sparkle Dish Detergent and discover for yourself what everyone is talking about!

• A car dealer looks directly into the TV camera and says, "If you don't get one of these year-end deals fast, somebody else will!"

    A. Bandwagon   C. Transfer
    B. Name calling   D. Glittering generalities

_____ 7. • A radio ad tells us: "Mom had struggled for years with lung disease—until we found Temple Medical Center. Now she's back home and doing all the things she loves—gardening, baking apple pies, taking walks with Dad, and keeping up with the grandchildren. Temple gave Mom her life back."

• An ad for Gold Medal Flour shows an ordinary-looking little girl and her grandmother making a pie crust.

    A. Testimonial   C. Bandwagon
    B. Glittering generalities   D. Plain folks

_____ 8. • A paper napkin advertises that it is "The common-sense napkin."

• A company offers a free sample of an energy-boosting pill. The television ad shows a woman in her sixties saying, "They're giving it away *free*? It *must* be good!"

    A. Testimonial   C. Name calling
    B. Glittering generalities   D. Transfer

_____ 9. • In 1961, the Freedom Riders were protesting segregation in the southern United States. The governor of Alabama appeared on television news and said that the protesters were "troublemakers and fools and Communist agitators."

• Why buy a gas-guzzler when you can get a luxury car *and* good mileage?

    A. Bandwagon   C. Name calling
    B. Plain folks   D. Transfer

_____ 10. • An ad encourages us to see a movie that "has warmed the hearts of all America."

• The sign in front of McDonald's proclaims, "Billions and billions served."

    A. Name calling   C. Plain folks
    B. Testimonial   D. Bandwagon

CRITICAL READING: Test C

A. Each pair of items below illustrates a particular error in reasoning. On the line next to each item, write the letter of the logical fallacy contained in both items. Choose from the three fallacies shown in the box below.

> **A** Circular reasoning *(a statement repeats itself rather than providing a real supporting reason to back up an argument)*
>
> **B** Personal attack *(ignores the issue under discussion and concentrates instead on the character of the opponent)*
>
> **C** Straw man *(an argument is made by claiming an opponent holds an extreme position and then opposing that extreme position)*

_____ 1. • Don't do that. It's against the law to do something that's illegal.

        • I've heard that the polar ice caps are getting smaller due to the fact that they're shrinking.

_____ 2. • Hayward would make a terrible president. He's been married three times.

        • Sheryl Hollin isn't qualified to be elected to the school board. She didn't learn to read until she was 14 years old.

_____ 3. • A candidate for mayor announces at a press conference: "Because I don't want this campaign to turn nasty, I will not mention my opponent's serious drinking problem."

        • This new treatment for AIDS was developed by a doctor who everyone knows is a lesbian. I don't see why we should invite her to speak at the medical conference.

_____ 4. • Mr. Upton signed a petition to stop using animals in medical experiments. He must enjoy hearing about people who die of cancer.

        • My mother doesn't want me to go to the party the night before my final exam. She doesn't care if I never have any fun.

_____ 5. • The longer we sit in this traffic jam, the longer it will take us to get there.

        • Sheila is a real chatterbox because she never stops talking.

(Continues on next page)

B. In the space provided, write the letter of the fallacy contained in each pair of arguments. Choose from the three fallacies shown in the box below.

> **A** False cause *(the argument assumes that the order of events alone shows cause and effect)*
> **B** False comparison *(the argument assumes that two things being compared are more alike than they really are)*
> **C** Either-or *(the argument assumes that there are only two sides to a question)*

_____ 6. • When I was a kid, we played simple board games like Monopoly and Scrabble, so I don't see why kids today need these expensive video games.

   • In Germany, there are no speed limits on their highway system. We should get rid of speed limits on U.S. highways.

_____ 7. • The new police commissioner isn't any good. He was appointed in June, and in August we had a rash of car thefts.

   • When hot chocolate sales go up, street crime drops. Therefore, hot chocolate must prevent crime.

_____ 8. • You ate only half of your dinner. You must not like it.

   • Are you against the war in Iraq, or do you support our troops?

_____ 9. • My sixty-year-old neighbor is crazy to be thinking about moving into a retirement community. After all, my grandfather power-walks every morning, drives his car, mows his own lawn, cooks for himself, and reads the newspaper every day.

   • The mayor said, "Many citizens are complaining that building the new power plant will increase pollution. But these same people are driving around in cars that cause pollution."

_____10. • It is obvious that these tax reforms pushed through by the mayor last spring are the reason the city's economy has collapsed this fall.

   • Charlene always carries her lucky penny when she has final exams. As a result, she has never failed a final exam.

CRITICAL READING: Test D

A. Following is a passage from a reference book. Identify each listed excerpt from the passage as either fact (**F**), opinion (**O**), or fact *and* opinion (**F+O**).

¹After four miscarriages, Lady Bird finally gave birth to two daughters, Lynda Bird and Luci Baines. ²Thus the entire family (including the dog, Little Beagle Johnson) had the initials L.B.J. ³With their parents constantly busy, Lynda and Luci were raised largely by hired help. ⁴As Luci commented candidly about her father, "Eventually, I learned to love him as a person, not as a father—because he seldom had time to be a father." ⁵Nevertheless, LBJ took great pride in his children, and in 1968 he announced, "I'm the luckiest man alive. ⁶Neither of my girls drinks or smokes or takes dope, and they both married fine men."

⁷During the White House years, Lady Bird established herself as the most influential First Lady in history, barring only Eleanor Roosevelt. ⁸Aboard her own "Lady Bird Special," she became her husband's most effective campaigner and helped win approval for "the Lady Bird Bill," a significant piece of highway beautification legislation that eliminated thousands of billboards and junk heaps.

_____ 1. Thus the entire family (including the dog, Little Beagle Johnson) had the initials L.B.J.

_____ 2. During the White House years, Lady Bird established herself as the most influential First Lady in history, barring only Eleanor Roosevelt.

_____ 3. Aboard her own "Lady Bird Special," she became her husband's most effective campaigner and helped win approval for "the Lady Bird Bill," a significant piece of highway beautification legislation that eliminated thousands of billboards and junk heaps.

B. Below are three items. On each line, write the letter of the main propaganda technique that applies to the item.

A Bandwagon	D Plain folks
B Testimonial	E Name calling
C Transfer	F Glittering generalities

_____ 4. In an ad for the Sleep Number Bed, a well-known television actress says, "Once you've found your Sleep Number, I know you'll discover, as I did, a deeper, more restful sleep. I actually sleep through the night now. . . ."

_____ 5. A handsome young man with sparkling blue eyes appears in an ad for contact lenses.

_____ 6. In a political speech, George H. W. Bush promised, "I will keep America moving forward, always forward—for a better America, for an endless enduring dream and a thousand points of light."

(Continues on next page)

C. In the space provided, write the letter of the fallacy contained in each pair of arguments. Choose from the three fallacies shown in the box below.

> **A** Circular reasoning *(a statement repeats itself rather than providing a real supporting reason to back up an argument)*
> **B** Personal attack *(ignores the issue under discussion and concentrates instead on the character of the opponent)*
> **C** Straw man *(an argument is made by claiming an opponent holds an extreme position and then opposing that extreme position)*

_____ 7. • Senator Rushmore wants to reduce air pollution. He must think we can get along fine without electricity and cars.

• My son's wife wants to get a job so they will have more money. She obviously does not care if the housework never gets done.

_____ 8. • A shopping mall has received complaints that it is starting the holiday season earlier every year. A spokesperson for the mall explains: "We know it seems like the holiday season starts earlier every year. But it's just that we start putting up the decorations earlier each year."

• I'm sorry I'm late for work, but it's because I didn't get here on time.

D. In the space provided, write the letter of the fallacy contained in each pair of arguments. Choose from the three fallacies shown in the box below.

> **A** False cause *(the argument assumes that the order of events alone shows cause and effect)*
> **B** False comparison *(the argument assumes that two things being compared are more alike than they really are)*
> **C** Either-or *(the argument assumes that there are only two sides to a question)*

_____ 9. • Anyone who refuses to recite the Pledge of Allegiance must not support our government.

• When you go to the grocery store, you have to choose between food that tastes good and food that is good for you.

_____ 10. • I don't see why women should work outside the home. My mother never did, and our family was perfectly happy.

• Why can't I have ice cream for breakfast? Jimmy's mother lets him have cereal for dinner.

COMBINED SKILLS: Test A

After reading the passage, write the letter of the best answer to each question.

[1]The general public may still think of Girl Scouts as pigtailed lasses who earn merit badges for learning to apply tourniquets to stop bleeding. [2]However, that image is dated. [3]Girl Scouts today are more likely to be talking about making career choices or dealing with sexual pressure than about building campfires or knitting afghans.

[4]In recent years, the New York City-based Girl Scouts organization has been bombarded with criticism that its programs were no longer relevant to today's young females. [5]In response, Girl Scouts began overhauling the merit badge programs and updating its guidebooks for members. [6]Drugs, sex abuse, and teen pregnancy are all topics dealt with in Girl Scout books published since 1987. [7]Girls today can earn merit badges reflecting current issues. [8]For example, badges are available for Girl Scouts who demonstrate their understanding of eating disorders such as anorexia and bulimia. [9]The result of these changes is that the Scouts organization helps members become more realistically prepared to deal with their lives.

____ 1. In sentence 5, the word *overhauling* means
   A. catching up with.
   B. improving.
   C. getting rid of.
   D. inventing.

____ 2. Today, Girl Scouts learn about such currently relevant issues as
   A. drugs.
   B. sexual abuse.
   C. eating disorders.
   D. all of the above.

____ 3. The relationship of sentence 8 to sentence 7 is one of
   A. contrast.
   B. time.
   C. illustration.
   D. comparison.

____ 4. The relationship between sentence 9 and the rest of the passage is one of
   A. illustration.
   B. comparison.
   C. cause and effect.
   D. contrast.

(Continues on next page)

_____ 5. The passage suggests that activities formerly associated with Girl Scouts include
   A. applying tourniquets.
   B. making career choices.
   C. understanding eating disorders.
   D. learning about teen pregnancy.

_____ 6. From the passage, one could conclude that
   A. Girl Scouts leaders were unconcerned by criticism of their organization.
   B. criticism of the Girl Scouts organization was unfair.
   C. most people preferred the old-style Girl Scouts organization.
   D. Girl Scouts leaders agreed that their organization needed updating.

_____ 7. Sentence 6 is a statement of
   A. fact.
   B. opinion.
   C. fact and opinion.

_____ 8. The author's main purpose is to
   A. inform readers about recent changes in Girl Scouts programs.
   B. entertain readers with surprising details about what happens in a typical Girl Scouts meeting.
   C. persuade readers that their sisters and daughters should join the Girl Scouts.
   D. predict that the Girl Scouts will soon become obsolete and disappear.

_____ 9. Which is the most appropriate title for this selection?
   A. Girl Scouts Changes: Too Little, Too Late
   B. Girl Scouts Change To Reflect Modern World
   C. The Girl Scouts Story
   D. Our Youth Learn About Social Problems

_____10. The central idea of this passage is that
   A. the Girl Scouts are an outdated organization.
   B. eating disorders are common problems among members of the Girl Scouts.
   C. the Girl Scouts have made changes to adapt to modern times.
   D. it is only recently that the Girl Scouts organization has truly served the needs of its members.

COMBINED SKILLS: Test B

After reading the textbook passage, write the letter of the best answer to each question.

[1]Many animals, including some insects, use visual clues to find their way. [2]For example, the female digger wasp lays eggs in a burrow in the soil. [3]She then flies off to capture her prey, which she stores in the burrow to feed her offspring when they hatch. [4]The famous animal-behavior scientist Niko Tinbergen studied the cues used by the female to relocate her burrow. [5]While the female was inside, Tinbergen surrounded the nest with pine cones. [6]When the wasp emerged, she flew around the nest before departing. [7]While she was gone, Tinbergen moved the cones about a foot away. [8]The returning wasp still sought her nest within the ring of cones. [9]Although the nest was in plain sight nearby, she was unable to locate it because the visual landmarks on which she relied had been shifted.

[10]Birds may also use landmarks, such as rivers and seashores, to find their way. [11]Several species migrate at night or over large expanses of ocean, using the position of the sun or stars to tell direction. [12]Many species seem to have genetically programmed information about the direction of the sun at various times of day, and also possess a biological clock that measures off a roughly twenty-four-hour day. [13]Other birds have the remarkable ability to "read" the night sky. [14]Indigo buntings, for example, seem to have a built-in star map that enables them to find which direction is north, during spring migration, by looking at the stars.

_____ 1. In sentence 4, the word *cues* means
   A. visual clues.
   B. movements.
   C. suggestions.
   D. lines.

_____ 2. The digger wasp used the pine cones as
   A. protection.
   B. food.
   C. a way to attract a mate.
   D. a marker by which to find her nest.

_____ 3. To find their way, birds may use
   A. rivers and seashores.
   B. the position of the sun.
   C. the position of the stars.
   D. all of the above.

_____ 4. The relationship of the second paragraph to the first is one of
   A. addition.
   B. time.
   C. contrast.
   D. cause and effect.

(Continues on next page)

_____ 5. The indigo bunting is a type of
  A. star.
  B. bird.
  C. insect.
  D. built-in star map.

_____ 6. We can conclude from the passage that the digger wasp gets its name from
  A. its shape.
  B. the person who first discovered it.
  C. the way it moves.
  D. the way it creates its nest.

_____ 7. The passage suggests that
  A. all animals have the same abilities.
  B. digger wasps can solve problems logically.
  C. birds have senses that humans do not have.
  D. all of the above.

_____ 8. Which is the most appropriate title for this passage?
  A. The Lives of Insects and Birds
  B. Telling Direction by the Sun and Stars
  C. Animal Parents
  D. How Animals Use Vision to Find Their Way

_____ 9. The central idea of the passage is stated in
  A. sentence 1.
  B. sentence 2.
  C. sentence 9.
  D. sentence 10.

_____10. The passage
  A. lists examples of the central idea.
  B. shows causes for the central idea.
  C. defines and illustrates a term.
  D. presents all of the major details in time order.

COMBINED SKILLS: Test C

After reading the textbook passage, write the letter of the best answer to each question.

[1]On the eve of Halloween in 1938, a twenty-three-year-old radio producer and actor, Orson Welles, broadcast his rendition of H.G. Wells's novel *The War of the Worlds* on the *Mercury Theatre on the Air.* [2]All week the cast had been struggling to adapt the story to radio and was finding it difficult to make the drama believable. [3]So Welles decided to present the story as an interruption of a regular music broadcast, with news reporters breathlessly cutting in to describe the landing of creatures from Mars.

[4]Although the broadcast included four announcements that the attack was just a dramatization, many people were listening to the Edgar Bergen and Charlie McCarthy show on another network when *The War of the Worlds* began. [5]During the first commercial on the McCarthy program, many people turned the dial to see what else was on. [6]They tuned in to an announcer describing a strange creature climbing out of a vessel in Grovers Mill, New Jersey. [7]Then they heard the announcer and a crowd of people being annihilated by the creature's ray gun. [8]National panic set in as people telephoned friends and relatives to warn them of the impending disaster.

[9]By the end of the hour-long broadcast, people had attempted suicide, jammed long-distance telephone lines and caused national uproar. [10]Military personnel were called back to their bases. [11]In Concrete, Washington, a power failure during the broadcast caused a traffic jam as most of the town's residents fled in their automobiles to escape the invading Martians.

____ 1. In sentence 1, the word *rendition* means
  A. memory.
  B. review.
  C. version.
  D. preview.

____ 2. In sentence 7, the word *annihilated* means
  A. eaten.
  B. destroyed.
  C. ignored.
  D. strengthened.

____ 3. Welles's radio show was based on a
  A. play.
  B. folktale.
  C. biography.
  D. novel.

(Continues on next page)

___ 4. According to the passage, the broadcast of *The War of the Worlds* included
   A. no commercials.
   B. four commercials.
   C. actual news reporters.
   D. four announcements that the story was fictional.

___ 5. The relationship between the two parts of sentence 5 is one of
   A. time.
   B. addition.
   C. contrast.
   D. comparison.

___ 6. The relationship of sentence 7 to the sentence before it is one of
   A. time.
   B. addition.
   C. contrast.
   D. illustration.

___ 7. The main pattern of organization of the passage is
   A. list of items.
   B. time order.
   C. definition and example.
   D. comparison and/or contrast.

___ 8. The passage clearly implies that the *Mercury Theater on the Air*
   A. was more popular than the Edgar Bergen and Charlie McCarthy show.
   B. wasn't very popular at all.
   C. specialized in science fiction.
   D. was broadcast nationally.

___ 9. We can conclude that many people felt Welles
   A. should never have tried to dramatize *The War of the Worlds.*
   B. should have appeared instead on the Edgar Bergen and Charlie McCarthy show.
   C. had no talent for radio.
   D. made the drama too believable.

___10. Which statement best expresses the central idea of this passage?
   A. A realistic radio drama about alien invaders caused national panic and uproar.
   B. Orson Welles presented a radio version of *The War of the Worlds.*
   C. Some people who tuned in to the *War of the Worlds* broadcast after it had already begun missed the announcement that it was just a dramatization.
   D. After a power failure in one Washington town, most residents fled to escape the Martians they thought were coming.

COMBINED SKILLS: Test D

After reading the textbook passage, write the letter of the best answer to each question.

[1]College classrooms are often drab and dreary places. [2]Walls are painted a variation of "institutional gray"; furniture is easy to clean, but uncomfortable and unattractive. [3]Chairs are lined up in straight rows facing the teacher's desk or lectern. [4]In one study, over 80 percent of university students rated their classrooms negatively, describing them as ugly, cramped, stuffy, and uncomfortable. [5]Research by environmental psychologists is beginning to show that unattractive classrooms are not only unappealing; they may also adversely affect academic performance.

[6]A carefully controlled study of classroom environments was conducted by Wolling and Montage (1981). [7]They selected two identical classrooms located side by side in the psychology building. [8]The control classroom, which they called the "sterile classroom," had white walls, a gray carpet, and rows of plastic desks. [9]The experimental classroom, which they called the "friendly classroom," was redecorated with the help of a design consultant. [10]Several walls were painted bright colors, art posters were hung on the walls, large plants were added to the room, and colorful Chinese kites were hung from the ceiling. [11]In addition to traditional desks, a part of the room was outfitted with area rugs, color-coordinated cushions, and wooden cubes to provide nontraditional seating.

[12]The researchers investigated how these two different environments affected performance in actual college classes. [13]Two professors teaching introductory psychology agreed to participate in the study, although they were not informed of the purpose of the research. [14]When school began, each class was randomly assigned to one of the two rooms. [15]Halfway through the term, the classes switched rooms. [16]Thus students in both classes spent half the term in the control room and half in the "friendly" room. [17]Students were not told they were being studied; the switch in rooms was explained as occurring because the original room was needed for videotaping.

[18]The most striking finding from this study was that students performed significantly better on regular course exams when they were in the friendly rather than the sterile classroom.

____ 1. In sentence 5, the word *adversely* means
    A. never.
    B. helpfully.
    C. negatively.
    D. playfully.

____ 2. In sentence 8, the word *sterile* means
    A. free of germs.
    B. empty.
    C. lifeless.
    D. safe.

(Continues on next page)

___ 3. The "friendly classroom" had
   A. bright walls.
   B. calm, pale colors.
   C. white walls.
   D. wall-to-wall carpeting.

___ 4. The students in the study
   A. helped design the "friendly classroom."
   B. took two different courses.
   C. stayed in one room throughout the course.
   D. were not told they were involved in a study.

___ 5. The main pattern of organization of the second paragraph is
   A. time order.
   B. definition and example.
   C. cause and effect.
   D. comparison and/or contrast.

___ 6. TRUE OR FALSE? Wolling and Montage's study was concerned with a cause-effect relationship.

___ 7. The passage implies that the "friendly classroom" was designed to be
   A. cheerful.
   B. informal.
   C. comfortable.
   D. all of the above.

___ 8. We can conclude from the passage that the two professors might have guessed the purpose of the study they were in because
   A. they had read about the interests of the two researchers.
   B. one of the two rooms they taught in was decorated unusually.
   C. someone gave them hints about the purpose.
   D. the study was done many times before.

___ 9. Which would be the most appropriate title for this passage?
   A. Traditional Desks versus Cushions and Wooden Cubes
   B. Sterile and Friendly Classrooms
   C. An Unusual Psychology Course
   D. Color in the Classroom

___10. The central idea of the passage is best expressed in
   A. sentence 4.
   B. sentence 5.
   C. sentence 7.
   D. sentence 17.

ANSWERS TO THE TESTS IN THE TEST BANK

VOCABULARY IN CONTEXT: Test A ✓

1. Examples: *paying the telephone bill, picking up the groceries;* B
2. Examples: *eating with my hands, being late everywhere I go;* B
3. Examples: *his car broke down, he lost his wallet, his computer crashed and he lost a day's work;* D
4. basic
5. requirement
6. shortage
7. Antonym: *wild;* A
8. Antonym: *poor;* C
9. D
10. A

VOCABULARY IN CONTEXT: Test B ✗

1. Examples: *watching travel TV shows, visiting faraway places on the Internet;* C
2. Examples: *keeps them from exercising, encourages them to eat unhealthy foods, teaches them to be violent;* D
3. outdated
4. wiped out
5. threat
6. Antonym: *silent;* B
7. Antonym: *hidden;* A
8. Antonym: *grow;* C
9. D
10. B

VOCABULARY IN CONTEXT: Test C

1. B		6. A	
2. C		7. B	
3. B		8. C	
4. C		9. A	
5. D		10. D	

VOCABULARY IN CONTEXT: Test D

1. C		6. A	
2. B		7. B	
3. D		8. A	
4. D		9. A	
5. C		10. D	

MAIN IDEAS: Test A ✓

1. 2		4. 1	
2. 1		5. 3	
3. 7			

MAIN IDEAS: Test B ✗

1. 2		4. 1	
2. 3		5. 2	
3. 5			

MAIN IDEAS: Test C

1. 2		4. 2	
2. 1		5. 1	
3. 7			

MAIN IDEAS: Test D

1. 2		4. 1	
2. 1		5. 3	
3. 6			

SUPPORTING DETAILS: Test A ✓

A.
1. D		4. C	
2. C		5. D	
3. A		6. Herbivorous (eat plants)	

B. (7–10.) *Main idea:* . . . categories of burn injuries.
1. First-degree—leave a painful red mark but do not break the skin so do not often become infected
2. Second-degree
3. Third-degree—outer and inner layers of skin are burned, causing little pain but possibility of serious or even fatal infection

SUPPORTING DETAILS: Test B ✗

A.
1. B		4. C	
2. D		5. C	
3. C			

B. (6–10.) *Main idea:* . . . genetic factors.
2. Intellectual traits
   Examples—scores on intelligence tests, memory
3. Personality factors
   Examples—shyness and special talents and interests

Note: Wording of main ideas and supporting details in Tests A–D may vary.

SUPPORTING DETAILS: Test C

A. (1–4.) *Main idea:* Psychologists use several theories to explain human behavior.
- Psychoanalytic theory holds that people are driven by "subconscious" needs and desires.
- Behaviorism suggests that people's actions are based on past experiences of reward and punishment.
- . . . the role of overall patterns in our thinking.

B. 5. 2   8. constructive
   6. B   9–10. A. Constructive forces, which
   7. C   lift up land masses
                          B. 1. Cutting action of running streams

SUPPORTING DETAILS: Test D

A. (1–6.) *Main idea:* A number of factors explain why poor people are less healthy than well-off people.
- Less nutritious diets
- Lower standard of living
- Less or lower-quality medical care
- Physical stress
- Psychological stress

B. 7. 1   9. B
   8. B   10. B

IMPLIED MAIN IDEAS: Test A ✓

A. 1. A   B. 4. D
   2. C
   3. B

IMPLIED MAIN IDEAS: Test B ✗

A. 1. B   B. 4. B
   2. C
   3. C

IMPLIED MAIN IDEAS: Test C

A. 1. B
   2. D
B. 3. Women use more flirting techniques than men do. *Note: Wording of answer may vary.)*
C. 4. C

IMPLIED MAIN IDEAS: Test D

A. 1. A
   2. D
B. 3. Several facts about the monarch butterfly are a mystery to scientists. *(Wording may vary.)*
C. 4. D

RELATIONSHIPS I: Test A

A. 1. after   B. 6. One
   2. until   7. Another
   3. next   8. during
   4. also   9. third
   5. Another   10. A

RELATIONSHIPS I: Test B

A. 1. B   B. 6. A
   2. A   C. 7. then
   3. B   8. As
   4. A   9. Finally
   5. A   10. B

RELATIONSHIPS I: Test C

A. 1. B   C. • Criminal cases that get heavy news coverage
   2. Soon *or* Eventually *or* until *or* then   • Other serious felonies that get less news coverage *Examples*—murders, rapes, robberies
B. 3. A   • Less serious felonies that may not get prison terms
   4. B   • Misdemeanors *Example*—traffic violations
  5–6. 1. They make and use tools.
        2. They eat meat regularly.

RELATIONSHIPS I: Test D

A. 1. A   C. 7. B
   2. In addition   8–10. *Main idea:* . . . five stages
B. 3. A   • Stage 3: Physical and psychological symptoms appear: illness, exhaustion, anger, depression.
   4. 1   • Stage 5: "Professional burnout" occurs: alcoholism, drug abuse, heart disease.
   5. Furthermore
   6. C

Note: In Tests C and D, wording of Part C answers may vary.

RELATIONSHIPS II: Test A

A. 1. for example   B. 6. A
     2. However   7. C
     3. reason   8. B
     4. Despite   9. A
     5. similar   10. C

RELATIONSHIPS II: Test B

A. 1. B   D. 7. B
     2. reason *or* causing *or* cause   8. result *or*
B. 3. C   effects *or*
     4. same *or* despite *or*   because
       differences *or* similar   E. 9. C
C. 5. A   10. opposite *or*
     6. for example   different

RELATIONSHIPS II: Test C

A. 1. C   C. 6. B
     2. B   7–10.
B. 3. A   • Seek to escape
     4. A   conflict at home
     5. C   • Overwhelmed by
                         demands of adult

Note: In Tests C and D,   life
wording of Part C answers   • Want to commit
may vary.   to establishment of
                         a better world
                     Main idea: . . . cults for
                     several common reasons.

RELATIONSHIPS II: Test D

A. 1. B
   2–4. *Main idea:* . . . common causes of a small
           business's failure.
            • Neglect
            • Weak control systems
B. 5. 1
     6. C
   7–10. *Heading:* Cities in Developing Countries
                 • Almost one half of population
                 • One quarter of work force
                    unemployed
           Homelessness

INFERENCES: Test A

A. 1. C   4. C
     2. B   5. B
     3. B
B. 2, 3, 4, 6, 8

INFERENCES: Test B

A. 1. A   B. 3. C
     2. C   4. B
C. 1, 2, 5, 6, 8, 10

INFERENCES: Test C

A. 1. C   3. B
     2. B   4. C
B. 1, 3, 5, 7, 8, 10

INFERENCES: Test D

A. 2, 3, 5, 7, 9, 10
B. 3, 7, 9, 10

PURPOSE AND TONE: Test A

A. 1. I   6. E
     2. P   7. P
     3. E   B. 8. C
     4. P   9. D
     5. I   10. A

PURPOSE AND TONE: Test B

A. 1. A   6. F
     2. G   7. D
     3. J   8. E
     4. I   B. 9. I
     5. C   10. P

PURPOSE AND TONE: Test C

A. 1. B   C. 5. B
     2. C   6. B
B. 3. A   D. 7. B
     4. D   8. A

PURPOSE AND TONE: Test D

A. 1. A   C. 5. C
     2. A   6. C
B. 3. B   D. 7. A
     4. C   8. C

ARGUMENT: Test A

A.
1. B
2. B
3. C
4. B

B.
5–7. A, E, F
8–10. A, B, E

ARGUMENT: Test B

A.
1. D
2. C
3. B

B.
4. D
5. B

ARGUMENT: Test C

A.
1–3. B, D, F
4–6. A, C, E

B.
7. C

C.
8. B
9. B
10. C

ARGUMENT: Test D

A.
1–3. B, D, E
4–6. A, C, F

B.
7. A

C.
8. C
9. D
10. C

CRITICAL READING: Test A

1. O
2. F
3. O
4. F+O
5. F
6. F+O
7. O
8. O
9. F
10. F+O
11. F
12. F+O
13. F
14. F
15. O
16. F
17. F
18. O
19. F
20. F+O

CRITICAL READING: Test B

1. B
2. B
3. D
4. C
5. C
6. A
7. D
8. B
9. C
10. D

CRITICAL READING: Test C

1. A
2. B
3. B
4. C
5. A
6. B
7. A
8. C
9. B
10. A

CRITICAL READING: Test D

1. F
2. O
3. F+O
4. B
5. C
6. F
7. C
8. A
9. C
10. B

COMBINED SKILLS: Test A

1. B
2. D
3. C
4. C
5. A
6. D
7. A
8. A
9. B
10. C

COMBINED SKILLS: Test B

1. A
2. D
3. D
4. A
5. B
6. D
7. C
8. D
9. A
10. A

COMBINED SKILLS: Test C

1. C
2. B
3. D
4. D
5. A
6. A
7. B
8. D
9. D
10. A

COMBINED SKILLS: Test D

1. C
2. C
3. A
4. D
5. D
6. T
7. D
8. B
9. B
10. B

Notes

Notes